D1120745

HETERO SEXUALITY

AMRIDGE UNIVERSITY LIBRARY

LIBRARY OF CONGRESS
AUG 30 1989
COPY
COPYRIGHT OFFICE

HETERO SEXUALITY

EDITED BY

GILLIAN E HANSCOMBE

AND

MARTIN HUMPHRIES

DIANA CHAPMAN
JOAN CRAWFORD
ROBERT GLÜCK
ALISON HENNEGAN
KRIS KIRK
SUNITI NAMJOSHI
ALAN WAKEMAN

KATE CHARLESWORTH
PETE FREER
NOËL GREIG
ROSANNA HIBBERT
AILEEN LA TOURETTE
JAN PARKER
JON WARD

Southern Christian University Library
1200 Taylor Rd
Montgomery, AL 36117

HQ
76.25
.H47
1987

control 14.709 record 169 disk 22

5666

First published September 1987 by GMP Publishers Ltd,
  P O Box 247, London N15 6RW
World copyright © 1987 GMP Publishers Ltd
Individual essays and illustrations
  world copyright © 1987 the respective authors
The Conversations of Cow by Suniti Namjoshi is published by
  The Women's Press

Distributed in North America by Subterranean Company,
  Post Office Box 10233, Eugene, Oregon 97440

British Library Cataloguing in Publication Data

Heterosexuality.
  1. Heterosexuality
  I. Hanscombe, Gillian E.   II. Humphries,
  Martin
  306.7'64   HQ23

  ISBN 0-85449-034-5

Printed and bound by Guernsey Press Ltd, C.I.

90-119563
02-16-90-EP30

Contents

Preface

Gillian E. Hanscombe

When David Fernbach of GMP first approached me with the idea for this book – that lesbian women and gay men might, for once, say something back to heterosexuals who have had such a very great deal to say to us – I teased him a bit. I said, 'I shan't search for international stars, you know. It'll just be me and my friends or friends of friends.' There was truth implicit in the tease, since at a serious level it was my view – and still is – that any one of us has something worth saying on the subject of heterosexuality, because whether we wish it or not, it's a subject we're forced to be expert about by virtue of merely living our lives.

Though I didn't seek stars, I do not mean to imply that any woman whose work appears in this collection is not – or may not become – a star. Nor do I mean to imply that I think the work appearing here is 'below' some 'standard' that professionals, on the one hand, or the literati, on the other, might apply. Heterosexuals after all, on the subject of homosexuality, rarely – if ever – stop before they speak in order to examine their credentials for describing us. I mean that I chose from among my friends or their friends on the basis that every one of them could write with authority on heterosexuality.

David and I easily agreed that I would seek and edit contributions from women, he from men. I wrote to friends – and friends of friends – suggesting that they might like to contribute a piece in a more or less light vein, since we were not intending to be scholarly in a rationalist way, nor wanting to be abstractly theoretical. I was astonished by some of the replies I received. I hadn't realised what pain and conflict the subject of heterosexuality could arouse in many lesbian women.

Many of us, for example, have been – or still are – married; and feel affection, kinship or just plain loyalty to male partners. One woman in this position wrote to me that she saw dangers inherent in a humorous approach, such that 'because They sneer at us, I don't see much validity in our descending to Their level and sneering at Them'. She went on to explain, more exactly: 'If I were to write a serious, albeit light, chapter on my personal experience of heterosexuality which gave way, after much turmoil, to my recognition of my lesbianism, it could not but cause distress to [my husband] and to my adult and my wholly heterosexual children. It is one thing working in the Gay movement and writing as an objective observer; it is quite another chronicling my struggle and the inevitable effect on my marriage for all to see. This may seem to you a total copout, and maybe it is, but I care deeply for the feelings of someone I have lived with [for so many years]...'

There are others of us who sometimes engage sexually with men. One such woman wrote to me: 'I don't feel I would be writing about heterosexuality quite from the outside – and that makes me feel ambivalent...The questions that do concern me about 'heterosexuality' are on the whole serious ones, such as the fact that other people...still assume that any heterosexual involvements 'cancel out' any lesbian ones and that relationships with men inevitably 'rescue' one from lesbianism! – a familiar attitude but still personally hurtful. I suppose what it comes down to is that the subject is something of a raw one for me at the moment.'

There were yet other women who felt unable to respond to my suggestion of humour or a light tone; the subject for them was anything but humorous. One who initially wanted to contribute gave up after several attempts, telling me that the process of hunting up her past heterosexual life had erupted each time in great rage and distressing nightmares. Another said she had many men amongst her friends and, while she had no wish to engage sexually with any of them, she nevertheless felt that to write the sort of piece it seemed I was requesting would be to engage in a 'them and us' polarisation which would be untruthful to her feelings and experience.

The seriousness with which these women responded to my request for a piece astounded me and challenged my own levity. Why had I responded without a trace of ambivalence to David's proposal? Did I welcome the 'them and us' polarisation where I ought more properly and painstakingly to assist in its dissolution? Was it merely a malicious glee I had in prospect when I saw how we might – at least this time – tell them how it is for us? Was I completely thoughtless about the bonds many lesbian women have with particular men?

Perhaps all this was true. But something else was also true. I held to my conviction, gradually and painfully realised through the work and lives of other women, that we do not live in a world of alternative sexual preferences, within which we cry out for acceptance as a misjudged minority. Such conditions may, for all I know, one day pertain, if a healthy society is ever brought into being. Meanwhile, I stand with Rich and other feminists, who explain that heterosexuality in this place and time is as learned and as institutionalised as 'democracy' or 'socialism' or 'scientific method' or – for that matter – 'literary standards'. It follows, then, that we are not part of a movement for equal rights, but that we are engaged in a struggle for change. Whether we will it or not, we are subversives, claiming by our existence and our utterance that heterosexuality is no more 'natural' than the feudal system ever was. Those who did agree to contribute to this collection make clear, in their different ways, that their views are similar.

I first met Rosanna Hibbert because she was Diana Chapman's friend and I had known Diana since the early seventies. I admire Rosanna greatly for many qualities. Not least among her battery of excellences is a formidable and trenchant wit, much in evidence in reviews she wrote for the original *Gay News* and for *Spare Rib*. She can be breathtakingly honest and quickly silence an entire roomful of women with some truthful observation or other. As she is professionally engaged in making television programmes for schools, I was pleased that she chose, for this collection, to write an address to teachers, who undertake, as she points out, a substantial share of the heterosexual training of girls.

Nevertheless, a 'training' in heterosexuality doesn't always work. It is common in this society for many of us to be 'treated', in one form or another, for madness: and for – irony of ironies – the cause of the madness to be diagnosed as lesbianism. Joan Crawford, for some years my esteemed literary agent and always a friend for whom I feel both love and gratitude, tackles this lesbian leitmotif of madness in a satirical psychoanalytic dialogue. Joan and I share the experience of psychoanalysis with many other middle-class lesbians from the New World, where we were not punished for sin, but were regarded with liberal dismay so profound that we accepted, or sought out, a treatment for sickness. We two mercifully became healthy lesbians rather than sick heterosexuals; but others of us have endured a much sadder fate at the hands of therapists whose therapies may differ but whose heterosexual preoccupations remain constant. (Another lesbian friend explodes the whole notion of such 'help' in two words: 'eschew psychobabble', she warns.)

Alison Hennegan, who became a loved and respected colleague when I joined the staff of the original *Gay News*, writes here with eloquence and acuity about some of her encounters with heterosexual domination. Her pain, made precise by her skilled use of narrative constraints, shows how the attitudes of heterosexuals can – and will, if not checked – so reduce a lesbian's provenance over her own judgements, so reduce the free emotional space in which she may conduct her social and personal intercourse, that she must either resist with rage or be pushed towards what heterosexuals call insanity. Either way she is faced with being silenced.

Suniti Namjoshi's contribution is extracted from a longer work, *The Conversations of Cow*, published by The Women's Press (1985). I met Suniti at the International Feminist Book Fair held in London in the summer of 1984. For a Lesbian Celebration evening held as a book fair event, she was one of a platform of readers whom I chaired. I was compelled to pleasure and admiration not only for her work but also by her reading of it. When I asked her for a contribution to this collection, she suggested the fourth section of *Cow*, which I agreed was eminently suitable, melding – as it does for me – a poet's instinct for irony with a lesbian's grasp of what heterosexual interchange is so often really about.

Diana Chapman and I met and became friends more than a decade ago, when Charlotte Wolff's *Love Between Women* was being published. Everyone in those days, including Charlotte Wolff, knew that if they wanted to know anything about lesbians in London they should go to Diana. She, after all, practically single-handed, initiated much of the lesbian network that those of us who came after now enjoy. It was she, back in the sixties, who responded to an ignorant piece of journalism about lesbians by writing a letter to a literary magazine. Replies to her letter led to the formation of MRG (Minorities Research Group); to Kenric; and then to Sappho: all many of us had until contemporary feminism arrived for us. Diana is one of our wise crones and is due more honour and attention than she would either permit or tolerate. But I very much wanted a piece from her for this collection; and she responded with an allegory. Here she too, though her roots are not in feminism, presents the lesbian woman as the one who is not subdued and who cannot be made to submit to heterosexual learning.

Because I was thinking about who to approach for contributors, Joan, who was then working as a literary agent, introduced me to one of her lesbian clients: Aileen La Tourette, who agreed to contribute. I find Aileen's piece beautifully balanced between poignancy, self-irony and insight: qualities which make clear how, for her, being a woman is a part in someone else's play, a role one must learn how to do and be, since it doesn't 'come naturally'.

I'd assumed at the start that some of the men's work would come in essay form, would be openly didactic; and that had been one reason why I'd so welcomed from the women such a diversity of styles: dialogue, anecdote, allegory, address, narrative and rhapsody, together with Kate's visuals. But it seemed, as time went on, that the men mightn't come up with a straight essay. I asked for a piece, therefore, from Jan Parker, whom I'd met at meetings about another book; whom I'd known through contact with the original *Gay News* and *Spare Rib* where she was a collective member; and who shared with me the experience of presenting a lesbian viewpoint to various parts of the intricate machinery through which the radical Labour Group was implementing Greater London Council policies. Jan agreed readily; and has spelled out succinctly and explicitly in her essay how urgent it is that heterosexuals get on with the task of examining the politics and stances of their conduct.

Kate Charlesworth's cartoons and drawings are widely known; but are particularly valued by every lesbian in Britain (and, I dare say, further abroad) who ever read a lesbian, gay or feminist periodical. She told me how surprised she'd been when she sat down to do the set of drawings that appear here; what surprised her was the range and extent of her anger. It's a justified anger; and appears so in each depiction of how heterosexual 'norms' have scorned, judged or otherwise rejected us.

What can we make of the themes these women present? There is Alison's hurt and anger that only heterosexuals may make proper judgements, make proper decisions, have proper reactions. There is Joan's witty and telling portrayal of heterosexual privilege, its manner and method of establishing such powerful norms that only a few, thus far, can withstand them. There's Aileen's pain at the knowledge of her heterosexual alienation, her perception of the 'otherness' of men, much vaunted by heterosexual tradition but seen by her as a subtle act of emotional withholding. There is the rage driving Diana's view that it is nothing less than herself that an acceptable woman is required to relinquish. There is Rosanna's proposition that heterosexuals are actually monosexuals: one-eyed people for whom heterosexuality is self-deluding, a shield which allows the most inordinate forms of self-indulgent subjectivity. There's Jan's challenge to heterosexuals to do their own thinking for the first time. There's Suniti's wryly observed presentation of mismatching and misunderstanding and – inevitably – mistrust.

What I make of these themes is partly conveyed to me by the women's use of their own experiences in what they write, showing – among other things – that the scarring we share as a result of living in a heterosexist world is something which prevents us from expressing cruelty towards our tormentors when we're given space to write and draw what we wish. The crude responses of theatre and pub audiences who are not in the least inhibited by belly-laughing at 'queers' and 'lezzies' seem barred to us.

More seriously, perhaps, is thrown up the difficulty we share in trying to establish a polemical mode in which heterosexuality may be openly attacked, rather than just challenged. Despite that difficulty, the openness of the modes these women have found is a positive result which others may feel able to build on.

Finally – and for me, most central of all – there is the awakening knowledge that beyond our political role as subversives lies our potential as visionaries. We are becoming capable, as we find our own voices and our own ways of telling things, of offering to anyone who cares to hear a more complete and more truthful description of what it is to be a woman than the descriptions of our unhealthy heterosexist culture have allowed us hitherto.

Southern Christian University Library
1200 Taylor Rd
Montgomery, AL 36117

Preface

Martin Humphries

My original involvement with this book was as one of the contributors, not as co-editor. In February 1983 I was one of a number of men who received a letter from GMP asking if I'd be willing to write something on Heterosexuality. I said yes. In April David Fernbach wrote to say that he'd taken on the job of co-ordinating the book, that eight men had shown interest and that the book would 'be rather loosely organised around its theme'. Articles were to be finished by August and publication was planned for the following year.

At this point I was thinking of writing a piece on advertising images and began making rough notes. In May David wrote again to say that the project had widened considerably and would now be the joint creation of lesbians and gay men. Gill had agreed to compile the women's contributions and together they would edit the book. Soon after this I talked with David about my ideas and through discussion decided to write something based on my personal experience rather than an abstract polemic.

I had been part of an all-male collective who produced a journal of anti-sexist men's politics and decided to write about my experience with them. I completed my first draft by September and sent it in. Although David acknowledged it I heard nothing further about the project. Later I discovered that the men's material was slow in coming together and that David had become overwhelmed by other work at GMP. Occasionally I'd ask him about the project but gradually it became forgotten as other work took over.

Then in April 1985, David told me that they wanted to try and complete the book but that the men's contributions remained unfinished. Would I read through these pieces and write a reader's report? I did. The eight contributions which existed at that time were varied in style, quality and length. Some had been written specifically for the book, others had not. I felt that several areas were missing and that the lack of thematic unity amongst the contributions highlighted the gaps. Having co-edited a previous book I was aware of the problems but felt that if some of the pieces were dropped, new ones commissioned and the remaining drafts completed we would have an interesting book.

David read my report and we talked. The result was that he asked me to take on the job of editing the men's contributions. I agreed. There were several reasons for this: I was excited by the book – particularly by the range and depth of the women's contributions; self-interest as I wanted to see my own piece in print; I had enjoyed co-editing *The Sexuality of Men* and felt more than ready to try my hand at another project.

First off I dropped two fictional pieces that hadn't been written specifically for the book. Then I wrote to all the existing contributors to let them know what was happening and asked if they were prepared to do further work on their articles. Two men decided not to continue with the project. This left me with four contributions. I then approached friends about writing new pieces for the book.

I asked Noël Greig if he would revise and expand an article on growing up which had appeared in *Achilles Heel*; he agreed. Pete Freer and I had often talked about AIDS and I knew he was giving a talk entitled 'AIDS for Heterosexuals' so I asked him to rework it for the book, again he agreed. I still felt that there was room for one more essay but here I met my first refusal. The friend I approached felt he had nothing to say about heterosexuality. He did consider writing an angry, personal, resentful piece about having a relationship with a married man and ending up dumped on by heterosexism but in the end thought this was a bad idea. His letter to me ended: 'When are the wretched hets going to start writing about it – as opposed to endlessly assuming it?'

I can see his point. It's only ourselves and some feminists who bring heterosexuality into question. Perhaps because we're always coming up against it? His saying this does indicate a different attitude/ experience from that of women; one of distance from those who define themselves as heterosexual. Gay men are not so commonly entangled in sexual/emotional relationships with heterosexuals – women or men. None of the men here have said anything about being married or being involved in childcare. As far as I'm aware we're men who knew we were gay from an early age. In the main our relationships with and to heterosexuality are via our upbringing and the fact that you can't get away from it in our society.

This divide is enhanced by our contributions: a fictional piece about one gay man's particular attitudes, two theoretical pieces and three describing past experiences and commenting on them. Yet, interestingly enough, all of them can be described as autobiographical – even the most theoretical is personally felt. A thread of ourselves runs through them all. It is as though this is the means by which we can begin to tackle or articulate our feelings about heterosexuality. Yet none of them is about one-to-one relationships. Being with groups of non-gay men; being brought up as though you're heterosexual; what to do when you take your boyfriend to meet your parents; the ways in which heterosexuals fear us and how they use that fear; an examination of their nature. All these things and more but not one is focused on a relationship with a specific individual.

All indicate that heterosexuality is a learned and institutionalised choice. This connects with the other, underlying, theme of change and the possibilities of change. Breaks in the walls, light on the subject, oxygen for the beleaguered! If we have anything to learn or to receive in return then acknowledgement of it is very muted. It would appear, most often, to be a one-way process in which we offer much. Much that is usually refused.

Whilst writing the above I continued to think about my own personal experience of heterosexuality and why I felt unable to write about those particular relationships. I identified one reason as a personal respect for those men and women who have continued to change. All the relationships were (are) difficult, problematic, even though in all of them I was (am) seen as a gay man. No, that is not specific enough. I have to separate this out further and here we hit the problem of definitions of heterosexuality. What is the essence of a gay man having a sexual/emotional relationship with a heterosexual man? Is it possible? Heterosexuals would say that that man was not one of them. Many gay men would say that he wasn't gay. He would probably be defined as bisexual! Having a relationship with him – and there have been several 'hims' in my life – cannot be said to be experiencing a heterosexual relationship except in terms of dealing with his attitudes and behaviour. In fact I've known gay men who've wanted me to be 'the wife'. Some gay men can be very heterosexual in their behaviour!

Yet for a gay man to write about his sexual/emotional relationship with a woman is extremely difficult. Even though this must be our most naked experience of heterosexuality. Not least in the way such a relationship is accepted by heterosexual society as against our usual circumstance of being people outside society. Maybe at some time in the future we'll be able to write openly about such relationships, but today we stand farther back and draw upon our histories with men or with society to illustrate what we think and feel about heterosexuality.

Despite the fact that the contributions came together over a long period of time and in a rather haphazard manner I think there is a general consensus articulated through the writing which connects to my own views. Crudely these are that heterosexuality is chosen – often imposed but nonetheless a choice – and that change is possible.

Kris Kirk's story is the most overtly humorous of the men's contributions. It details the effect misconceptions and bigotry about heterosexuality have on one gay man. Although the characters are fictional 'Derek's' do exist. In this story it is Derek who needs to change or else he may find that his parents have left him behind.

Coming out is important for the possibilities it offers not only to ourselves but also to our parents and friends.

Pete's essay on AIDS has as its starting point his own feelings of fear and anger. Fears about AIDS itself and anger at the ways in which the media have manipulated those fears. The media have targetted us as the canker within society that is now receiving its just deserts. As Pete makes clear, AIDS affects heterosexuals and they too will be forced to adjust their behaviour. In fact the sooner they make changes the safer we'll all be. In the meantime we have to devise our own public and private strategies based on our own needs rather than in response to heterosexual demands.

One hope for the future is working with heterosexuals in political groups. My own essay on the four years I worked with Achilles Heel is a mixture of autobiography and comment. At times it was exasperating working with a bunch of men who, for all their good intentions, were often reluctant to do their own work in examining their heterosexual prejudices and conditioning. Yet one irony is that I wouldn't have edited this book if I had not gone through the experience of working with them.

Robert Glück's journal is also, on one level, about the experience of being with heterosexual men in a political situation. He is an American writer, living in San Francisco, who was arrested on an anti-nuclear blockade on June 20th 1983 and held for eleven days with 'mainly straight John Does of conscience' plus guards and authorities. His journal of those eleven days has as a subtext the fears and desires of many gay men towards male heterosexuals. Gay men often have an ambivalent relationship with non-gay men that is based on the power held by the latter. Such power can be attractive to gay men and we have to work out our relationship towards it. At one point he says 'in one week I recapitulate my entire maturation'. Throughout he clearly expresses the stress of being held captive, with others, for one's beliefs, as well as the stress of being one of the few gay men in that particular situation. Ultimately it is a moving and uplifting piece but it does indicate the distance heterosexuals will need to travel before change has any reality.

Noël's essay on the stratagems used when he was sixteen to hide his gayness, yet also allow it some life, is concerned with the stresses placed upon us by heterosexual society. Some of us emerge from adolescence intact. Others never make it. Some of us remain damaged for years. As he says, 'It is a wrong sort of world where young people have to learn habits of shyness and deceit in order to survive.' How many parents, other than ourselves, are prepared to validate the homoeroticism of childhood? Education authorities certainly won't. In 1983 Devon Education Authority banned Gay Sweatshop's production of *Poppies*. In 1985 Perspectives Theatre Company's produc-

tion of *Best of Friends* – a play about a family that has some gay
characters – was banned by Nottinghamshire Education Authority.
These bans were imposed despite the fact that schools and the pupils in
them wanted to see these productions. Mind you, it is in the nature of
'authority' to refuse to accept more than one sexuality.

Pete Freer briefly mentions the concept of 'Nature'. In his essay Jon
Ward explores this concept thoroughly in an incisive and invigorating
manner. In this essay he sees the concept of nature as one which
appears at the crux of the sexual conflict. Taking us through the social,
philosophical and historical construction of the term he articulates this
conflict. The tentative conclusion is one suggestion of a way in which
the prison of heterosexuality can be unlocked. I'm pleased that we
included this essay which extends the boundaries of the current
debate. No doubt it will cause controversy – at least I hope it will!

The fact that this book expresses the thoughts and feelings of
lesbians and gay men is a positive virtue. The men's contribution totals
six essays. Where does it get us? The overwhelming feeling I get from
the men's writing is that the 'single role' of heterosexuality is
completely spurious. By single role I mean the perception and
presentation of heterosexuality as a single entity. The one *valid* way for
human beings to be. Within this 'heterosexuality' men and women are
seen to join together in harmonious union, whilst anything outside of
this unit is seen as deviant. In fact I think we are very noble in
indicating, quite clearly, the variety of means of expression open to
heterosexuals, particularly in terms of the possibilities for change. Our
generosity extends to crediting them with a future. This is not a
facetious remark. Many of our feelings are raw yet here we present
considered views and weighed opinions. Scorn and bitterness are
tempered with a benevolence of spirit. Perhaps, yet again, we are in the
forefront and in years to come, as changes occur, such generosity will
be reciprocated. This is a slender hope but to my mind it shows that,
despite everything, we still have a vision which is open to all and shared
by many.

What Exactly Is Heterosexuality...and What Causes It?

Alan Wakeman

Heterosexuality is a condition in which people have a driving emotional and sexual interest in members of the opposite sex. Because of the anatomical, physiological, social and cultural limitations involved, there are formidable obstacles to be overcome. However many heterosexuals look upon this as a challenge and approach it with ingenuity and energy. Indeed it can be said that most heterosexuals are obsessed with the gratification of their curious desires.

WHAT EXACTLY IS HETERO-SEXUALITY ?

...& WHAT CAUSES IT ?

HORMONAL IMBALANCE?

One theory advanced is that heterosexuals have an imbalance in their sex hormones:- instead of the normal mixture of the two, they have an excess of one or a dearth of the other, resulting in an inability to enjoy full and satisfying relationships with their own sex.

ECONOMIC CONDITIONING?

FEAR OF DEATH?

Our society grants financial and other incentives for exclusively (i.e. neurotic) heterosexual coupling: from tax concessions to council houses. To be gay is expensive and many people simply cannot afford it.

A terror of mortality lies beneath much heterosexual coupling. Driven to perpetuate themselves at any cost, most heterosexuals are indifferent to the prospect of the world-wide famine that will result if the present population explosion continues unchecked.

PARENTAL PROBLEMS?

In most cases of compulsive heterosexual behaviour, the parents will be found to have suffered from similar difficulties.

CHILDHOOD TRAUMA?

A bad experience with a member of the same sex while young may cause rejection of all members of the same sex through fear. The desire continues in the subconscious and emerges as a heterosexual neurosis.

SOCIAL CONDITIONING?

Many unthinking heterosexuals succumb to the daily bombardment of conditioning from the mass media and live out their lives trapped in oppressive stereotypes. We should feel compassion for such people, not hostility, for their rejection of all those parts of the self that do not conform to the 'married-couple' ideal, is a measure of their loss of contact with their own unique sexuality.

PATHOLOGICAL CONDITION?

Many heterosexuals claim that they were just 'born that way'. Unfortunately this doesn't hold water. All human beings are the result of the interaction between their substance and their environment and heterosexuals, like the rest of us, must share in the responsibility for their condition.

CULTURAL DEPRIVATION?

Most heterosexuals will be found to have come from a background in which an appreciation of the beauty of their own bodies has been ruthlessly suppressed. Heterosexual men in particular think themselves 'ugly', beauty being ascribed only to women. Many psychic disorders stem from this self-rejection.

Teacher Training

Rosanna Hibbert

I must make my position clear. Four statements will do it. One: I think that hetero-sex is rather disgusting – but I am not proposing here (nor would I ever attempt) to tell people that they shouldn't do it; my disgust is only important to me and has nothing to do with this case. Two: I know that, physically, heterosexuality can be highly delightful for women and men but I am sure that, socially and politically, it is usually disastrous for women. From this comes my third statement: the state of being heterosexual is an aspect of women's struggle for equality which is not enough thought about. Fourth: I have not got the breadth of imagination to address myself effectively to the men's side of this issue, so I propose to blast away at a body of people which is largely female – except, naturally, in the higher echelons – namely school teachers.

Heterosexuality often starts when you are very young. If you are a girl it can, like it was said masturbation used to do, make you blind. Worse, though, than this, it can make everyone else blind to you – in fact it almost always does. It is these three things about it (not my disgust, which I hope I have put in its place) which convince me that it is urgently necessary for teachers to realise that being heterosexual is a political act. What is more, unlike strictly 'political' lesbianism, female heterosexuality is usually involuntary and therefore its young practitioners need help if their political awareness is to be fully aroused.

Now the trouble about being political (of course you realise that I am not talking about Parties, but about Life) – the trouble is, it is a rather grown-up thing. Your average person may not understand what it is to act politically until they first cast a vote; this they will associate with Parties. Their consciousness, be they young women or young men, will need to be raised above the level of their parents' habitual voting patterns, which will be entirely governed by Parties; inevitably, because the candidates they have voted for have always been Party-goers and nothing at all to do with Life. These candidates have also been predominantly men (who invented Parties and love going to them, particularly if they last all night in Parliament). Somehow we have to give politics the kiss of Life. We must do this for all our sakes, but mostly for the sake of heterosexual women, and the only way to do it is to catch them young and grow them up quickly. This is what schools are for.

Of course I know that schools are forcing houses for stereotypical heterosexuality. 'Boys *will* be boys,' say the staff grimly. 'Girls bloody well *will* be girls. Heads will roll else.' And the teachers – most of whose heads are men – give science and woodwork and attention to the boys, and social studies and typing and ignore-ance to the girls, and the world spins safely on with nary a wobble. But not all teachers are trimmers; some of them are not even heterosexual: the road from subversion to salvation for women runs past the door of the Staff Room. Unfortunately teachers, if they are any good at all, already work extremely hard, so why do I want to lumber them, not the parents of the children they teach, with this extra load? (And it will be a heavy job, teaching Life politics, because it is part of every single bloody class you take, whatever other subject you're meant to be on about.) Shouldn't the kids' parents be the ones to beat Life sense into them? Of course they may help, but teachers have got to do the bulk of the work because they are handling large units of children. They are in the middle of the mob, and Mob Rules OK, there's no doubt about that. If a schoolgirl is lucky and convinced, she can just about be a closet Life politician at home; but in the playground and the classroom she will find it terribly hard to come out and stand fast; and only if she is exceptional will she emerge at 16, or even 18, with a clear view of heterosexuality and the training to cope with it. All girls must receive good teaching and ample support right there in Mobland, otherwise they will become blind, invisible and wasted.

Feminism is the nearest we have got to Life politics up to now, and I know from work I have done making television programmes for use in schools, that there is a growing feminist movement among teachers – mostly among the women, with a sprinkling of token men. I have observed that in a good school – that is, a vigorous, politicising and critical place with a stimulating atmosphere in at least one corner of the Staff Room and a head who is at least complaisant – the fight for sexual equality is joined by both staff and girls. (Yes, it *is* a fight, even in a good school, and the rearguard actions from the entrenched staff and pupils of both sexes can be strong enough to feel like cavalry charges.) I have also seen that the struggle, the uprising, which is being attempted by at least as many heterosexuals as by people of other persuasions, has to storm the same heterosexual walls which, up to now, the rebellious have thought of as home. It is a Civil war, in fact. The young troops, the girls, may be excused for not realising this only if you also excuse the ignorance of their Staff Officers.

I must be careful here. I started by begging teachers to teach; but I seem to have got us into a war mode, and you might say that it is not fair to expect effective instruction when everyone in the classroom is shit scared that the next bullet will have their name on it. The time has come for me to make my fifth statement to add to the four I began with. I am a member of the fair sex and a Libran to boot; for these reasons I know that, although my campaign puts great demands on people, my cause is great: it is nothing less than fairness to my sex and we may well have to bust our guts to get it.

So, teachers, to your siege machines! That is to say, watch your language. Words are our essence and our only weapons, yet how many of you use words which teach girls anything they don't 'know' already? The sexist use of language in teaching and textbooks is no new subject: the dearth of women in 'history'; the male orientation of maths and science exercises; the attention paid to boys in class; their precedence, the amount of room they take up; the use of 'man' when 'human' is meant; the praising of meekness in girls and aggression in boys – all this excrement amounts to a massive buttressing of male bastions, and you will say, as you hold your nose, that you are fully aware of it. I do not think that you are. This linguistic reinforcement of received heterosexuality is so strong that it amounts to a toppling even of that cause. Until you revise your language and the attitudes which derive from it, and rewrite your textbooks, you must be considered not only anti-feminist but also monosexual.

Who could imagine themselves actually owning up to monosexuality? It is patriarchy run mad, and it is monstrous. I suspect that most monosexuals hide their proclivity behind a mask of heterosexuality. I also suspect that – because of this – there are many more monosexuals around than you realise. Hence the witless reinforcement of heterosexuality even by people who think that they are thinking, such as 'feminist' teachers. I have been to conferences, seminars, courses, meetings of anything from tens to hundreds of teachers who want to do something about sexual equality but I have never heard the issue of heterosexuality discussed; as the monosexuals know, it is *not* an issue. It could be, and I can think of one way of making it so. All teachers who are *homo*sexual could come out. What a dream: the world put straight by bents! And you must not misunderstand me here. I am not now doing what homosexuals are so often accused of; that is, trying to convert everyone to my kind of sexuality. I want recruits to the army as a whole, not to a particular regiment, and I refuse to let you think that I'm after press-ganging everyone to the gay colours. I am making a serious point: that declared homosexuality brings real and feigned heterosexuality into the open, where it should be.

Two encounters I have had made me think like this. Both of them happened in secondary schools but this does not let primary teachers off my hook – particularly as so many of you are women. It is never too early to start teaching female children the rudiments of Life politics, and of all teachers, you who work in primary schools and who are generalists in the profession, are best suited to cast a Life-like glow across the curriculum.

I remember taking part in an 'Equality Week' at a London comprehensive. On the day I was involved, women and men who had jobs which could be seen as unusual for their sex spent the time talking with small groups of 14 to 15-year-old girls and boys. We were meant to be thought-provoking. I spent the day in a large classroom where four or five of us moved between groups of up to ten kids. I encountered about 50 teenagers this way and provoked not a single thought. By the end of the day – what would be tea-time in any normal person's life – I was knackered. I attribute this bruising humiliation to three things. First, myself: I am not a stereotypical 'TV Producer'; that is to say I am middle-aged and not at all flash. Nor am I a reliable teacher of groups; if the eight or ten faces around me don't warm to me I cannot always glow. I seem utterly to have failed, all day, to make my work sound challenging, interesting, or even odd for a woman to do, in spite of the rightness of the first two descriptions and my growth out of the fear that the third might be true. Second, the school: the pupils appeared not to know why the speakers were there nor why they had been pushed in to endure us. Third, heterosexuality: the rabidly conservative, male-biased political heterosexuality of the uneducated young. One group I faced up to included an edgy boy who stirred up his male mates and could not look at me. But suddenly he did. 'Are you a *feminist*?' he said, and on the word scraped his chair out of the circle. It was extraordinarily violent. It sums up for me all of men's investment in heterosexuality and their loathing and fear of women. The boy seemed impermeable and frightening. But none of the girls scared me; they were all simply depressing. At 14 or 15 they were already lobotomised: they could decide to sit together; they could chew gum; they could giggle at the boys or me; and that was it.

There were not enough feminists on the staff of that school and I assume that any there had minimal support from management. In this case the fight had only just started and the troops had been drafted in without training. (What irony! Man, the butch fighter who proves his masculinity by his aggressiveness, sets up wars when he has good stocks of arms and disciplined manpower. Kudos results, win or lose. Woman, wanting to argue but discovering that man likes battle better, will 'scramble' armed only with her convictions. What's more, her heterosexual feminine credibilty has gone forever – particularly if, astonishingly, she wins.)

I remember another incident at a school I went to when I was researching for a 'women's studies' series which I wanted to make. I was looking for ideas, reactions to my ideas, and substantiation of my feelings about the need which I thought existed. The marvellous feminist cobweb which I discovered during my research led me to this particular school; that is to say it was an established point of feminist teaching. Here I came up against a far more sophisticated attack – and in a younger class too. The children were 13 to 14, more girls than boys; I was with them, without a teacher, for one period; they had been well-briefed. There was one boy – brightish, middle-classish – who obviously felt attacked by the female talk which had been crackling across the gaps. He had the wit and the experience not to get at 'Miss' but at the girls; he made diminishing comments on their contributions and demanded a lot of my attention. He used his heterosexuality far more subtly than my London boy had done. 'Fuck you,' to a teacher, is rude but irrelevant: 'You're slags,' to your female peers, over whom you already have considerable power, works. For bonus points, it also puts visiting 'Miss' on the spot.

What I thought at the time of both these incidents and have thought since is, should I have come out to these two lots of schoolchildren? Few, if any, of them can have been knowing and acknowledging homosexuals themselves; even so, would an announcement of my non-heterosexuality have done something to reinforce the feminism which I was trying to bring to their attention? It might have got the girls thinking positively in a small way, even if only in private, or together after I had gone, particularly in School Two. But it could very easily have set all the boys off chasing lesbians. I can imagine my chair-scraper in School One, consumed by heterosexual aggression, rising and shouting to the rest of the room that he was having to listen to a fucking dyke. How would the giggling, gum-chewing girls have reacted to that? Would their femaleness have been reinforced? Or would they have felt threatened?

I guess that the latter would have been much more likely. And as I look back, that guess justifies my shrinking violet self. But when I look forward, I know I was wrong. I failed to teach; I colluded with heterosexuality to protect young females from male scorn in spite of the fact that I believe such protection actually amounts to disablement and premature death of the spirit. By hiding my homosexuality I was also, of course, protecting the boys from the dreadful fact that the world would go on wagging for me and my sisters, and wagging very merrily too, if men had never been invented.

Good teaching is the opposite of protection: it makes life perilous for children; but it gives them the skills to see the dangers and a relish for hunting out ways to handle them. The politics of heterosexuality is the most dangerous subject which girls ever have to learn; it is therefore the most challenging to teach. I am asking all heterosexual teachers to acknowledge this, and all homosexual ones to confront it. Our schools spew out hundreds of thousands of blind and invisible human females every year with a complacency which appals me.

The Media Giving the Public What It Wants

Hetiquette

(a plain man's guide to passing for straight)

Kris Kirk

The Adelphi Hotel
Scarborough
October 1st

Dear Robert,

My little heart-throb! I do hope you're over that little row we had just as I was leaving London and that you've calmed down a little. It's very important indeed that you're on your best behaviour when you meet Ma and Pa this weekend! Oh, Roberto, what bliss – a whole weekend together at my folks' pied-à-terre in Didsbury. Perhaps not the most romantic of places for a quasi-honeymoon, I'd agree, but I'm sure we'll have a memorable time. As long as you're not going to continue nagging me about my being discreet with the parents, that is.

It quite put the wind up me, our row. I'd already begun to realise that some of those lefty college friends of yours take great pleasure in flaunting their queerness and shouting it from the rooftops, but I was shocked at the degree to which you appear to share their feelings. I thought you were a nice boy and that, like me, you *cared* about the feelings of others.

Because, you know, that is why I am as circumspect as I am with my nearest and dearest. I take your point about paranoia and perhaps I am too worried about mother having a heart attack, but I was aghast at your suggestion – put so strongly if I may say it – that my parents don't assume that I'm 'normal'. I presume you were joking when you marched off in a huff saying I was as camp as a row of tents. You obviously haven't seen me in my leathers.

What I took greatest exception to was your inference that all I'm worried about is that Pa will cut me out of his will if he discovers I'm bent. Of course it would be lovely to inherit what little they have – must be about 10 grand now – and it wouldn't be natural if I wasn't concerned about alienating them, but that is a secondary, minor consideration I assure you. As I've endlessly spelt out to you, my great worry is mother's heart. It's all very well for you to say she's as strong as an ox and battled through the Blitz, but I just couldn't live with myself if I induced a coronary.

Anyway I'm pleased you've deigned to 'go along with the subter-fuge' as you so gracelessly put it, and I promise it won't be as difficult or embarrassing as you so gloomily predict. I grant that my not being able to get away from the Alliance bash in time to pick you up and drive us both to Didsbury will add unforeseen difficulties. Particularly as you stormed off when I tried to prime you a little about how to comport yourself with mes parents and now we won't have the opportunity of a journey to run through our 'alibis' as you call them. But as there were only a handful of things I had to spell out to you, I shall do it now. I must insist however that you commit to memory *every* point I mention.

First and foremost WE DO NOT LIVE TOGETHER. As I've said before, as far as my parents know I live alone waiting for the right woman to come along. There's no need to disabuse them of their ignorance and we must be careful not to do so by mistake. I don't quite know what you meant when you accused me of patronising them and we'll have to discuss that in a free moment, but until then you're an old pal from school who I met up with again at...let's say...a football match. I know you're as ignorant on that score as me (ha!) but I'll check through some Sunday papers to find out a ground near where I live and which team plays there, and perhaps we could bluff our way through recounting the match we saw.

Before you leave home, remember to be VERY CAREFUL as to what you put in your suitcase. Mother was once told that a good hostess always unpacks her guests' suitcases for them, so for God's sake leave behind *anything* that may cause suspicion. Obviously KY, poppers, porn and your Gay Men's Diary are OUT but be sure not to bring the *towelling* dressing-gown (father may think it sissy) and only pack a bare minimum of toiletries (after-shave and deodorant are okay nowadays, I suppose, but not body-rub. It *sounds* so suggestive). And for God's sake remember to bring your own sponge-bag – we don't want them to think we share toothbrushes.

Clothes are always a problem. I would have recommended that leather jacket of yours as suitably butch, but if they've seen Freddie Mercury on the telly they'll know now what a leather queen is. Also they're mad on travel programmes so they might have seen *Cruising* on the telly by mistake; after all, they sat through *Dr No* thinking it was a sequel to *Doctor in the House*. The leather is out then, but if you search through the very back of my wardrobe you'll find an old Gannex mac of mine which should do the trick. It's not the most flattering garment in the world and you'll have to put up with Harold Wilson jokes, but at least it's safe. And it's not as though you'll have any reason to want to look sexy this weekend, is it?

Of course skimpy underwear is out too – the baggier the Y-fronts you pack the better. You may think they will never be seen but I'm sure other people notice knicker-lines too. And leave all your white socks at home, please – they might be regarded as effeminate. We have already had a little contretemps over your earring and I take the point that even the butchest Rugby League players wear them nowadays. But I'm not sure if that fact has filtered up to sunny Didsbury yet, so I'm afraid it'll have to go. The hole in your ear is a give away of course, but we'll just have to hope that my parents' eyes aren't as sharp as they were. As to the rest of the clothes you pack, it's very simple really – nothing too scruffy (otherwise they might want to know why I mix with a ragamuffin!) but nothing too smart either – we mustn't let them get the impression that you're effete!

Can you also remember, darling, to take the silver ring off your little finger? I've already removed mine. I know you think other people don't notice things like that, but better to be safe than sorry. And do be sure to bring an extra thick towel. I don't suppose for a moment there'll be any opportunities for grunties, but if the folks *were* to go out for a guaranteed couple of hours, we would certainly need something to lay over the bottom sheet. I couldn't bear the embarrassment of trying to explain a stain. The thought brings me out in a sweat.

I just can't understand why you insist on travelling up to Manchester by coach when I have already offered to fund your travelling First Class by BR, but as this 'independence' stance of yours has been the cause of a lot of friction entre nous recently I shan't pursue the point. And, as it happens and no thanks to you, it makes the whole sorry question of your arrival a little easier.

Obviously it's essential that I'm on hand to effect the introductions: it would be hideous if you arrived in Didsbury on your own because I'm sure they'd grill you and discretion is not, after all, your strong point. In fact I have timed things perfectly so that I'll be at home in Didsbury when your bus pulls into Manchester. But as there is an outside chance of yet another dust-up between the two Davids which could just delay my arrival, I've worked out a foolproof plan.

When you arrive at the coach station, ring home and make sure I'm definitely there. If I'm not, explain to mother – for some reason father never answers the phone – that you're NOT at the coach station but that you're phoning from a motorway service station because the coach is running late. Keep all explanations to a minimum. After you've rung off you'd better give it an hour before you ring again – we don't want them to think you're an hysterical weed – and if I'm there I'll come and pick you up. Otherwise you'll have to keep stalling. There is at least a tea-vending machine in the station and with a bit of luck the waiting-room will be open. But whatever you do, *don't* contemplate calling a taxi and coming over alone – we will need the journey time in the car to work out the details of how we met etc, and it will be our last opportunity for me to test you on our 'alibis'.

When we get there, I'll do the introductions. I don't think I need to ask you to give father a good firm handshake, but for continuity's sake please remember to do the same with mother. They may compare notes. I also think it would be best if you kept as silent as possible, to make sure you don't say something incriminating. If you're asked any leading questions, be vague. And in case you're absolutely forced into answering a difficult question, I suggest we work out some kind of system of signals. I'll scratch my ear if the answer to their question is 'yes', and if it's 'no' I'll stroke my chin. That should be easy enough for you. And remember that sometimes the most innocent questions are often the most dangerous ones. Never admit, for example, that you know how many sugars I take in my tea. Things like that suggest a degree of intimacy and – for this weekend – we are NOT intimate.

I've never known an evening when mother hasn't spent most of it slaving away in the kitchen so she shouldn't be too much of a problem to deal with, though don't do anything gallant like offering to help her in there because she may just use the opportunity to pump information out of you. Anyway I'm sure she will expect us to spend the evening with father, who is going to be the main problem. The poor old stick often makes an attempt to discuss how I am and what I'm up to, but as that's the last thing I want to talk about with him I'll try to get him to talk about darts or something butch like that. BBC2 runs a late night programme on darts doesn't it? Must try to catch that and brush up on the terms. And *please* don't let him know you're on the dole. I take your point that as half the North is out of work nowadays, the folks are probably more tolerant of scroungers than I am, but I don't want to risk *anything*, so keep your lip buttoned. You seem to know plenty of permanent students so it shouldn't be too difficult for you to pretend to be one of them. Say you're doing research in sociology or something – ha!

After dinner mother will probably suggest a spot of telly and as she knows that politeness is the subordination of oneself to others – a dictum you would do well to learn – she'll no doubt invite you to select our viewing for the night. PLEASE be extra-careful in what you choose. Avoid light entertainment programmes like the plague; I couldn't bear to sit in their company watching either Inman, Grayson or Kenneth Williams doing their thing or any of those madly hetero comics who always seem to end up wearing a frock. Speaking of which, if Hinge and Brackett are on then I'm afraid mother might slyly suggest we watch them. I've never managed to work out whether she knows they're not real women, but perhaps we can assume they're safer ground than either soap operas or human interest documentaries – it's astonishing how often a certain 'sensitive subject' pops up in both.

All in all, if I were you I'd plump for a wildlife programme if there's one on, even though we're certain to be bored rigid by it. And if by any hideous chance they run an item on AIDS on the news just *stay silent*, as I will. If you *are* obliged to comment just nod and *don't* roll your eyes if I say something you disagree with. Remember we are not going there as envoys from the gay world or as educators, but as guests of people from a different generation than ours.

If things begin to get troublesome, you'll have to feign a headache and go to bed early; it's better to run the risk of their thinking you're a weed than to make some almighty faux-pas. At least you'll have a nice, comfortable double-bed to go to – I'll be sleeping on the couch. I can't imagine *anybody's* parents suggesting we share a double bed but even if mine did I would decline; it could be their way of testing us out. Besides, we might be tempted by grunties, and I'd be mortified if we made the slightest squeak. In fact you must try to restrain yourself completely all weekend. But if you *have* to relieve yourself make sure you do it safely, like into a sock.

At least we should wake up fresh as daisies on the Saturday morning for my cousin's wedding. Tricia's marriage is to be a formal 'do', of course, so at least you'll be able to sit with a book and watch us all running round like headless chickens, with me in my topper and tails! Much as I'd love to have you in the second-to-front pew with myself and my parents, I know you'll understand that such a thing just isn't on. Indeed I'd say that the nearer the back of the church you sit, the less discussion you'll provoke. Mother is a sentimental soul and she may try to persuade you to sit with us, but I'm sure you realise this would probably set the whole family's tongues a-wagging and we don't want *that*, do we?

The wedding breakfast afterwards may be more tricky, I'm afraid, as I won't be at the same table to guard and protect you! I will, however, try to ensure that you're placed next to the people who will give you the least trouble. This will mean very elderly aunts or uncles and/or toddlers I'm afaid, but though their company won't be exactly gripping at least their interrogations won't be as astute as certain other members of my extended family.

One other piece of advice: if anyone asks you 'Are you courting?', just stare into your soup and blush. If you do that for long enough they'll presume you are but are too lovelorn to admit it. And one further thing – do avoid getting into deep conversation with my Uncle

Charlie. In everyone else's eyes he may be a happily married man with five kids, but he has been making passes at me since I was 12 and he's hardly likely to remain untempted by you. Beware the wandering hands.

Because of the wedding mother might have already got in the provisions for the weekend so, with a bit of luck, we might avoid the usual ghastly Saturday afternoon shopping excursion. But if we do have to trudge to Tescos, remember that we are on hand to carry the groceries, not to twitter over the price of avocadoes or to swap cheesecake recipes with mother – *that's* hardly likely to impress father.

If Tescos is out then we'll be staying in on Saturday afternoon, getting ready for the big dinner. I notice *The Rains of Ranchipur* is the Saturday matinee movie, but I'm afraid we'll miss out on you cooing and gushing over Lana Turner because father and I like the Saturday afternoon sport. Well of course I don't, but I've always encouraged him to think I'm gripped by it all. If your ignorance of football is as legion as I suspect, it might be worth your while swatting up on all the teams on a pools coupon beforehand. That should give you enough knowledge to busk your way through the afternoon.

I do hope mother won't be in a panic about dinner. My parents aren't used to entertaining and I'm afraid it was me who persuaded them to invite the Simpkins over. Father isn't a particularly ambitious person and has never made any effort to impress old Simpkins, which is stupid really as it's in the latter's gift to have dad manage a bigger modern furniture showroom than he's responsible for now. Anyway, now that I've put the squeeze on there's a chance the two will get chummier, though father has always had what I've felt was an incomprehensible coolness towards the chap.

I'd guess you'll probably have similar feelings, though I have to admit I rather admire Simpkins' nerve – he's a real go-getter. Type of bloke who always has a wheelchair standing by for him when he lands at foreign airports on a business trip. Not that he's crippled of course – it's just a ruse for getting through customs quickly. I'd have to admit his wife is a bit of a snob and we'll *all* have to watch our step with her. Her way of distinguishing whether or not one is top-notch is to rub her finger over one's visiting card to see whether it's engraved or just printed. I don't suppose you'd even know what a visiting card is, would you darling?

Anyway, you can see why it's extra important that you remember your table manners. If mother serves cherries remember to remove the stones *unobtrusively* from your mouth; if you eat an orange don't forget to use a knife to remove the peel. And above all, *do* try to remember that we sometimes have to be pleasant to people we don't want to be pleasant to. For everyone's peace of mind, please don't start trying to discuss serious subjects and embarrassing us all in the process: that's *not* what a dinner party should be about. Just try to be polite. Without being *too* polite, of course, and seeming like a sissy.

Even mother is au fait enough to know that two women and four men on such an occasion is an impossibility, so she'll have invited two other women. I guess they will be my cousin Michelle and her 'friend' Julie. I've been convinced for years they are lesbians, but of course, I've never dared approach the subject with Michelle because that would involve revealing my own proclivities which, as you know, is just not on.

You'll probably get on with them, given that they're as bolshy as you are turning out to be: I just hope and pray you all have the grace not to egg each other on to start discussing controversial subjects. For that reason I must ask you to watch carefully what you drink – of course I'll keep a friendly eye on you. I'm sure you'll have the good sense not to talk about sex, but for God's sake please avoid politics too. I warn you now that the Simpkins are rather the Moseley and Mitford of Didsbury whilst Michelle and Julie seem rather lefty – I remember them once being rather patronising towards me when I once suggested that there's no such thing as class any more in this country.

I rather think putting the four of them together is asking for trouble, but as long as you and I keep out of such conversation we should survive unscathed. I always remember as a child reading something very wise, I thought, by Barbara Cartland of all people. She was addressing the hostess, but I think it's a dictum that equally applies to guests too: 'A good hostess has no time at her own party for prolonged conversation', it's so true.

Sunday is church again, I'm afraid, but I'll give you a quiet prod each time you have to kneel and stand. There's no reason, after all, why mother and father should find out we are neither of us regular churchgoers. After that, mother will have to get home quickly to prepare lunch, but I don't want you to try skiving off with her instead of coming to the Catholic club with father and me. Father does most of his business deals there; says he's never bothered to join the Freemasons because he's in the best masonry in town! Then off for a spot of lunch and it'll all be over. I warn you now that I may be a little upset as we drive away from Didsbury – sometimes I think the life we live in London is a little sterile compared to the richness of family life.

Anyway m'dear, that's enough of the deep philosophy! I'm looking forward terribly to seeing you on Friday and I bet you're gettng excited too. Do you know you're the first lover of mine I've ever taken home? I did invite Richard once and we were all set to go, but he caught that awful contagious virus which meant he had to stay alone in his flat for weeks and weeks. In fact it was that which induced the terrible depression in him which finally finished our relationship off. We never actually made it up to Didsbury together. I do hope the same thing won't happen to you! Only joking of course! See you very soon, my angel.

Lots of love from your

Derek X

P.S. Please don't give my parents' number to anyone – I don't want any of your piping friends squawking down the phone at mother. And please burn this letter – I would just die if mother came across it in your suitcase.

P.P.S. Do remind me to ask you what you meant by that strange remark you made as you were racing out of the door – about how you were never a political creature until you met me. Don't say I'm beginning to convert you to the cause!

Whose Problem Is It Anyway?

Joan Crawford

Introduction

When Sigmund Freud first formulated his psychoanalytic theories he was attacked for challenging many taboos and customary ideas. However, despite the seeming radicalism of his work, he was deeply rooted in the prejudices and philosophies of his historical period and class. Certainly in the subsequent development and institutionalisation of his theory and methods, the general social outlook of the psychoanalytic profession has been highly conformist. And nowhere has this been more telling than in its approach to homosexuality. Unlike most of his contemporaries, Freud neither repudiated it as a sin, denounced it as a crime nor classified it as an illness; but, on the other hand, he did view it as evidence of arrested sexual and emotional development. His followers established much more firmly than Freud had ever done that homosexuality was a seriously pathological condition: for them, homosexuality resulted from arrested psychological growth; attractions to one's own sex were residual infantile or adolescent fantasies; persistent homosexual activity indicated emotional maladjustment. This view prevailed until the mid-1970s when, under pressure from new theories of cultural construction, together with the assertiveness of the Women's and Gay Liberation movements, a substantial part of the psychotherapeutic establishment began to question the notion of homosexuality as an illness. In 1973 the American Psychiatric Association removed homosexuality from its diagnostic manual of mental disorders. However, the influence of such a formal decision is slight and it is still frequently the case that those with homosexual leanings presenting themselves for psychoanalysis are considered sick. Admittedly, many people, unable to bear the isolation and discrimination that being homosexual in a predominantly straight society entails, have gone to analysts asking to be 'cured' of their homosexual feelings in order to be relieved of their social outcast state. Analysts have then colluded with the distressed person's view of her or his orientation, thus reinforcing the individual's sense of guilt. The possibility that homosexuality is a viable alternative and that people can lead rich and fulfilling lives in partnerships with members of their own sex, is hardly considered. Clearly this has more to do with the profession's obsession with social normalcy than with empirical evidence.

Given this background it seemed an amusing exercise to imagine a period in the indeterminate future where the situation is reversed; homosexuality has become the norm, heterosexuality the minority pathology. What follows is an imaginary account of the psychoanalysis of Mandy, aged 20, who has entered into treatment with Dr Lillian Carewell.

For those unfamiliar with the procedure of psychoanalysis a few explanations may be helpful. Ideally the patient visits the analyst for an hour a day, five days a week, for a period of upwards of two years. The patient lies on a couch; the analyst sits in a chair behind the patient, out of sight. The patient is encouraged to 'free associate', that is, to say whatever comes into her or his mind at random. The analyst avoids choosing the subject under discussion, but asks probing questions to help the patient explore more deeply what has arisen. The patient's free association is interpreted by the analyst in the light of her or his theoretical knowledge. Reactions to the analyst are also analysed, the theory being that the patient will replicate in her or his relationship with the analyst those emotional blocks which are interfering with relationships in general. The procedure is known as 'analysing the transference'.

What follows are some excerpts from Dr Carewell's records, the first extract dating from the first year of the analysis.

*

Mandy:	But supposing I *am*...*(anguished pause)*
Dr Carewell:	*(solicitously)* Yes...
Mandy:	*(trembling)*...h e t e r o s e x u a l *(gasp of horror)*
Dr Carewell:	That was very brave of you, Mandy. It's difficult to say the word. But it's important when we're trying to confront our feelings.
Mandy:	But I didn't want to say the word. It feels awful. I feel as if just by saying it I'm admitting that's what I am.
Dr Carewell:	Do you think it will alter my feelings towards you?
Mandy:	I don't care what your feelings are towards me.
Dr Carewell:	*(indulgent laugh)* So we're back on that tack today, are we?

Mandy:	Yes, WE are. WE are getting a bit pissed off with YOU bringing everything back to yourself. I was telling you what I felt about Terry and next thing I know you're rabbiting on about yourself again.
Dr Carewell:	*(the acme of patience)* Mandy, do you think there might be some significance in the fact that the name 'Terry' can be both a girl's name and a boy's name? Do you think your choice of Terence, whom I should point out you always refer to as Terry, is an expression of your confusion in this area?
Mandy:	*He* always refers to himself as Terry. Anyway, I didn't choose him. He chose me. He's *made* me feel certain things towards him that I don't want to feel.
Dr Carewell:	But Mandy, that's what you're always saying about me – that I'm trying to make you feel things about me that you don't want to feel.
Mandy:	Yes, but in his case he's succeeded whereas you haven't!
Dr Carewell:	Perhaps it's more difficult for you to allow yourself to feel things towards me.
Mandy:	Why would it be? I came here asking to be cured of these feelings I have for Terry. I want to be a normal homosexual just like everybody else. If I'm attracted to the opposite sex then I'm a freak, an outsider. If I had feelings towards you I'd be quids in. First of all I'd be on the road to happy homosexuality and, secondly, I'd be achieving a transference (which I do realise, by the way, is what all this ME ME ME stuff of yours is about) which would mean that the therapy was 'working'. So what possible reason would I have for denying feelings I'm dying to have?
Dr Carewell:	Maybe it's more threatening to admit you have feelings towards me. After all, the implications are considerable. If you were to release your true homosexual feelings then you would have to face things like getting married, raising a family, taking your place in society etc. As long as you persist in these

adolescent heterosexual feelings you can avoid all that.

Mandy: I'm not exactly bursting to take my place in

Dr Carewell: *(silence)*

Mandy: *(silence)*

Dr Carewell: *(silence)*

Mandy: You're trying to get me to say something.

Dr Carewell: *(silence)*

Mandy: Well, I'm not going to.

Dr Carewell: *(silence)*

Mandy: So there.

society. As a matter of fact I'm not at all impressed by the organisation of family life at the moment: the requisite two same-sex children rationed by the state, rotating employment with one partner one year, the other the next, total 50/50 split of earned income between the two partners, regardless of their earning power. At least with them both individuals can work all their lives if they want to and keep their own income.

Dr Carewell: But they can't have children, can they?

Mandy: Not at the moment, no. But there is a pressure group among the 'merries' (I gather you know they call themselves that to distinguish themselves from the drab uniformity of homosexuals)...

Dr Carewell: *(says nothing)*

Mandy: Anyway, they're lobbying to be allowed access to the sperm banks. Also, you never know, we might have a revolution one day and men wouldn't automatically have the operation any more. It seems unnatural that they should.

Dr Carewell: What do you think *is* natural, Mandy?

Mandy: I don't know.

Dr Carewell: Do you think sex between women and men is natural?

Mandy: I don't know.

Dr Carewell: Do you think a couple of a woman and a man could make ideal parents for a child?

Mandy: It used to be considered acceptable.

Dr Carewell: I asked you whether *you* considered it acceptable?

Mandy:	I'm not sure.
Dr Carewell:	Do you want to be heterosexual, Mandy?
Mandy:	That's a bit like asking someone whether they want a hare-lip. Nobody actively *wants* to be a member of a persecuted minority.
Dr Carewell:	Mandy, maybe I can point out to you what has happened. Earlier in the session you were talking about your own feelings and your feelings for Terry. When I tried to show you the connection between your feelings about yourself and your relationship with me you became involved in abstract intellectualising about society. Now you and I could easily get tucked into a nice cosy argument about the organisation of society, but I wouldn't really be helping you with your feelings about yourself, now would I?
Mandy:	*(rather desperately)* But aren't those things important?
Dr Carewell:	Of course they are. But they are of secondary importance to your feelings about yourself.
Mandy:	*(even more desperately)* But doesn't one shape the other?
Dr Carewell:	To some degree, yes. But you must allow your feelings to come through first. Once you've got those out in the open we can worry about the other questions later.
Mandy:	*(defeated)* Oh, all right.
Dr Carewell:	*(silence)*
Mandy:	Shall I tell you what happened the other night?
Dr Carewell:	Certainly.
Mandy:	Terry rang me and suggested we go out for a drink. He told me the fellow he was supposed to be seeing had to go to a meeting of his local houseworkers' union and he was feeling at a loose end. We had a drink at the Nag's Head and then walked back through the park. I asked him about Frank – that's the guy he was supposed to be seeing – and he said Frank had gone to visit his fathers in Essex. I looked at him and realised he'd lied on the phone, or he was lying now. Then he realised what he'd said and we both just stared at each other...

Dr Carewell:	*(silence)*
Mandy:	And...
Dr Carewell:	Umhum...
Mandy:	He looked so handsome. I know that must sound like a funny thing to think about a man – when you're a woman – but I just couldn't stop looking at him and...
Dr Carewell:	Umhum...
Mandy:	*(intense embarrassment)* I wanted to touch him.
Dr Carewell:	Where?
Mandy:	His face. He looked so embarrassed and uncomfortable.
Dr Carewell:	Did you want to touch him anywhere else?
Mandy:	Like where?
Dr Carewell:	I was just enquiring.
Mandy:	You want me to say his thing, don't you?
Dr Carewell:	I don't necessarily want you to say anything in particular.
Mandy:	*(slowly)* I've often wondered...you know...what it looks like. His thing...what it feels like to touch...*(clams up)*
Dr Carewell:	What do you imagine it would feel like?
Mandy:	*(silence)*
Dr Carewell:	Why have you stopped, Mandy?
Mandy:	I'm not enjoying this.
Dr Carewell:	It's important.
Mandy:	Why?
Dr Carewell:	As you know, Mandy, a man's thing, his penis, becomes erect when he is sexually stimulated. Under these conditions it becomes very powerful. And the thrusting movements of the penis in the male rectal passage in normal male homosexual love-making can appear rather violent. Now, we all have some awareness of this from a variety of sources – mainly cheap pornography. What we do know is that often in the early stages of the psychosexual development of the female child the penis becomes the source of masochistic fantasy. The girl child imagines herself to be attacked by the potent male member and punished for misdemeanours – real or imaginary. Full, mature, female sexual development is marked by a loss of interest

	in these infantile fantasies and an identification with one's own sex and the rich, tender, gentle love-making which is the hallmark of lesbian love.
Mandy:	But what about men? Are you saying they are all masochists?
Dr Carewell:	Not at all. The penis doesn't engender the same fantasies in men because they all possess one. Also men are more genitally focussed, whereas the nature of the female physical response is more diffused – the way in which women achieve orgasm involves touching, stroking and fondling over the whole body. That is basically why women prefer their own sex.
Mandy:	I know all that and I know it's wrong but what I feel for Terry doesn't feel wrong. *(pause)* I felt *protective* towards him. I didn't feel frightened at all.
Dr Carewell:	Yes, but don't you see, Mandy, that what you are expressing there is the classic emotion of nurturance which women in our society feel towards each other. This is the pre-genital stage of sexual encounter which is the most satisfying aspect of lesbian love. If things had developed between you and Terry you would have passed into the next phase of sexual contact in which your infantile masochistic fantasies would have been stimulated. I would have to argue that this element was present in the encounter although you suppressed your awareness of it.
Mandy:	*(silence)*
Dr Carewell:	I would also suggest that you allowed yourself to feel what are essentially healthy normal homosexual feelings with a man because you knew that if a sexual encounter took place you would be overtaken by your infantile masochistic fantasies thereby protecting yourself from experiencing the true opening and union which you could achieve with another woman.
Mandy:	Why the hell would I do that?
Dr Carewell:	Because it is frightening. When two women

or two men have true sexual congress there is
a surrendering of the self. For reasons we
have yet to explore you find this deeply
threatening.

Mandy: But I've made love with other women – lots
of times. You know that. It's OK. I have
orgasms, but I don't feel close to them.

Dr Carewell: Well, I think it's important we talk about
that. However, I think we're going to have to
leave it there for today.

Six Months Later:

Mandy: *(silence)*
Dr Carewell: *(silence)*
Mandy: I can't speak. My jaw's locked.
Dr Carewell: *(silence)*
Mandy: God, you don't believe in making it easy for
people, do you?
Dr Carewell: You want me to take responsibility for guid-
ing the session in a particular direction. Then
you can say that that was *my* choice, thereby
relieving you of the responsibility of
determining what we're going to talk about.
Mandy: But you guide the sessions anyway – surrepti-
tiously – by the loaded questions you ask. At
least if you were more out front about it I'd
know that you were making me go in certain
directions. As it is, the technique is so
devious that I can be persuaded that I'm
talking about things because I want to,
although the truth is that you've got me to
talk about them without appearing to.
Dr Carewell: *(silence)*
Mandy: *(pounding her fists on the couch and shouting)*
I HATE YOU!
Dr Carewell: GOOD, Mandy!
Mandy: *(screaming)* I HATE YOUR SMUG SELF-
SATISFACTION! AND I HATE YOU
MOST OF ALL BECAUSE I KNOW
YOU WANT ME TO SAY I HATE YOU.
AND I DO BUT NOT FOR THE REA-
SONS YOU THINK.

Dr Carewell:	*(calmly)* Why do you hate me, Mandy?
Mandy:	Because you're BBBBOORRRRR-RINGGGGGGGGGG!
Dr Carewell:	Perhaps you think you're boring yourself, Mandy?
Mandy:	Oh, I give up. I should know by now that I can never win at this game.
Dr Carewell:	Why do you think you keep coming to see me, Mandy?
Mandy:	Because I'm unhappy. But I could be plain ordinary unhappy. I might not be unhappy because of my sexual feelings. I might be unhappy just like hundreds of other normal maladjusted homosexuals.
Dr Carewell:	*(silence)*
Mandy:	I guess I may as well tell you what happened. *(long silence)* I...slept...with...him...
Dr Carewell:	Terry?
Mandy:	Of course it was Terry. Who the hell did you think I meant – the head of the Fathers' League?
Dr Carewell:	*(silence)*
Mandy:	*(lies rigidly with her fists clenched and her jaw locked. Begins to shake violently thrashing her head from side to side and kicking the couch)*
Dr Carewell:	*(silence)*
Mandy:	*(bursts into wild screaming crying. She flings her arms uncontrollably and fights madly for her breath)* I feel so AWFUL...I feel so DIRTY...I couldn't face my mothers. I can't face anyone. I feel like such a *FREAK*.
Dr Carewell:	*(silence)*
Mandy:	*(gradually calming down)* I told you he was going away to this new job in the West Country. Well, he rang me last night and said he discovered, while packing his things, some of my books. (We'd always exchanged books – we seemed to find the same things interesting.) He suggested I came round and collected them. When I got to the house there wasn't anyone else there. I thought that was a bit strange but he gave me a drink, we started talking and I forgot. We just talked

and talked and I didn't notice the time. I
guess we had a lot to drink as well. I can't
really remember how it happened. One
minute I was sitting in the chair and the next
minute I was with him.
*(stops and starts crying again. This time she
cries quite freely, the tears streaming down her
face)*

Dr Carewell: How did you feel, Mandy?
Mandy: *(sobbing violently)* Everything happened so
                 fast. My body seemed to race ahead of me.
                 I've never had that feeling before. With
                 women I've always been a spectator.
Dr Carewell: Did Terry penetrate you?
Mandy: *(silence)*
Dr Carewell: *(silence)*
Mandy: *(covering her face, nods her head convulsively)*
Dr Carewell: Do you feel ashamed, Mandy?
Mandy: *(nods her head convulsively again)*
Dr Carewell: Where you frightened when he penetrated
                 you?
Mandy: Yes...well, I'm not sure. I was frightened by
                 all of it. My heart was pounding away like an
                 old sledgehammer. My body was doing all
                 these things and my mind was racing. I kept
                 thinking: he's not a woman, he's a *man*. I
                 can't be doing this. I just kept staring at his
                 body. With women they're *like* you, they're
                 the same. It all seems so natural. But men
                 are so *different*.
Dr Carewell: Yes, Mandy.
Mandy: Finally I just got up and put my clothes on
                 and left. I can't remember what I said –
                 something silly about I hoped the job worked
                 out.
                 (silence)
                 When I walked back my legs were like jelly –
                 I could hardly make them go. I looked back
                 up to his window and saw he'd put the light
                 out. And you know what I thought? I
                 thought: I want to go away with him. I want
                 to live with him. And then I thought: But I
                 can't. He's not a woman. What would people
                 think? What would they say if we walked

down the street holding hands. They'd laugh and sneer and say horrible things. Then I felt so awful. Someone passed me in the street and I wondered if she could tell just by looking at me that I'd slept with a man. Then I felt as if I'd never be able to look anyone straight in the face again. That everyone would look at me as if I had a disease. I thought: Now I'll never be able to be with a woman. I couldn't ever tell anyone, they'd never understand, they'd just think I was a MONSTER. Oh, what am I going to DO? *(starts crying again, desperately).*

Dr Carewell: Do you think I think of you as a monster, Mandy?

Mandy: YOU MUST.

Dr Carewell: I think you think of yourself as a monster, Mandy.

Mandy: Well, I must have got that from somewhere, mustn't I?

Dr Carewell: Mandy, let me try and show you what's happened. At the beginning of this session you were very angry with me.

Mandy: I was angry because you wouldn't help me.

Dr Carewell: Precisely. You've had this very distressing experience with Terry and you need the understanding which one woman can give to another woman. At *that* moment you chose to tell me that you hate me. You hated me at that particular moment because you so badly needed me to love you. Now, supposing I were to show you the kind of caring you crave for in those circumstances, how do you think you would react?

Mandy: *(perplexed)*

Dr Carewell: I suggest that you would feel a very natural inclination to reciprocate.

Mandy: You mean I would love you back?

Dr Carewell: Something like that, yes.

Mandy: But I've been loved by another woman. Beth never stopped telling me she loved me – practically drove me round the bend.

Dr Carewell: Yes, but Mandy, you didn't really expose yourself to Beth – you didn't reveal your

	inner feelings to her. So you didn't really put her proclaimed love to the test, did you?
Mandy:	Given the nature of my inner feelings, I don't think that would have been such a hot idea, do you?
Dr Carewell:	But you have revealed your inner feelings to me. Just at the moment that you're going to tell me about a most upsetting experience, you say you hate me. I submit that what you really mean is that you love me.
Mandy:	*(shouts)* BUT I DON'T LOVE YOU, I LOVE TERRY! *(hears what she has said and bursts into floods of tears again)*

Excerpt From Dr Carewell's Notes:

The session continued rather unsatisfactorily along these lines. The neurosis is obviously more deep-seated than I realised. The poor girl was dreadfully upset by her experience with Terry – I did what I could to relieve her guilt but she is extremely masochistic. Of course, quite understandably, she is totally denying this aspect of the encounter. It's quite clear from what she told me that fear of punishment plays a major role in her attraction to him but she is very resistant to seeing that.

One Year Later:

Mandy:	Good morning, Dr Carewell. How are 'we' today?
Dr Carewell:	I'm fine, Mandy. How are you?
Mandy:	OK, I suppose. Well, not really. But if I say it often enough I might believe it.
Dr Carewell:	*(silence)*
Mandy:	Carol and I went to a party last night.
Dr Carewell:	Yes...
Mandy:	I must say it's nice going places together. Everybody was there in couples – Anne and Sue, Frieda and Felicity, Karen and Gillian. We just waltzed in and chatted about our jobs, our plans for the holiday, all that. I thought: This feels really *normal*, just like my mothers and their mothers before them. And,

you know, people treat you differently when you're with another woman – you just swan around basking in their approval. It's almost enough to convince you that you *are* happy.

Dr Carewell: Mandy, you've come a long way in the time we've been together, particularly in the last year. But you can't expect a lifetime of emotional difficulties to evaporate overnight. Now when you came in today you asked me how 'we' were. It is quite clear to me that you now think of us, you and me, Mandy, more and more as a couple. That's a very encouraging sign.

Mandy: I was just making a stupid joke, that's all.

Dr Carewell: Well, Mandy, stupid jokes, as you call them, have their roots deep in our subconscious.

Mandy: *That* particular joke has its roots deep in a book called *Good Morning Miss Dove*.

Dr Carewell: *(silence)*

Mandy: *(silence)*

Dr Carewell: *(silence)*

Mandy: You don't read much, do you?

Dr Carewell: What would you have me read, Mandy?

Mandy: Well certainly not *Good Morning Miss Dove*. But novels, yes, and plays, poetry.

Dr Carewell: These things do have a certain interest in revealing the psychopathology of their creators but I find case studies a more instructive way of examining personality disorders.

Mandy: But people who write books and plays and poetry don't *think* they've got disordered psychopathologies. They think they're looking at the world with new perceptions, different perspectives...

Dr Carewell: *(silence)*

Mandy: Books can change the way people see the world!

Dr Carewell: Mandy, I *must* point out to you that you're getting off the track again.

Mandy: I think I'm very much on the track.

Dr Carewell: Let's look at it this way, Mandy. You started by telling me about the party you and Carol had been to. You said how good it felt to be together and how much you enjoyed yourself.

	Then you deliberately went back to your old habit of intellectualising. But that's what it is, Mandy, a *habit*. What I'm trying to do is help you to learn new habits of being happy.
Mandy:	But I said it was almost enough to convince me I was happy. I didn't say I was happy.
Dr Carewell:	None of us are a hundred per cent happy all the time, Mandy.
Mandy:	But I was happy being accepted by other women, feeling I was really one of them because I had a woman lover. That was the main thing. I mean, I'm really fond of Carol, she's nice and all that. I feel really guilty that I can't seem to love her the way she loves me.
Dr Carewell:	But you have grown to care about her more and more.
Mandy:	Yes, I guess so...
Dr Carewell:	Well...
Mandy:	Well, what?
Dr Carewell:	Have you any reason to assume that that process won't continue?
Mandy:	*(unconvinced)* No, I guess not.
Dr Carewell:	Well...
Mandy:	I find her kind of boring. She's nice but I don't feel 'at one' with her, so to speak.
Dr Carewell:	We don't always feel at one with other people. Sharing one's life with another woman involves a certain amount of tedium in day-to-day chores, responsibilities etc. But part of the process of growing up is accepting those rather dull patches and not allowing them to mar the moments of shared happiness.
Mandy:	But what I'm saying is that I don't think there are moments of shared happiness. Companionship, yes. Social status, yes. But no real closeness.
Dr Carewell:	It will come, Mandy.
Mandy:	*(silence)*
Dr Carewell:	*(silence)*
Mandy:	*(hesitantly)* Something happened at the party.
Dr Carewell:	Yes...

Mandy:	Judy was there with her, lover, June. She's been living down in the West Country for the last six months. She told me she'd seen Terry.
Dr Carewell:	*(silence)*
Mandy:	He's married. To a guy called Mike.
Dr Carewell:	*(silence)*
Mandy:	When she told me, my stomach lurched. I just stood there shaking and trying not to show that I was upset.
Dr Carewell:	*(silence)*
Mandy:	When Carol and I drove home I couldn't talk to her. I just sat there like a mummy. And when I finally got to bed at home I just cried and cried. *(she starts to cry now. She weeps inconsolably until she is exhausted)* It just feels like great waves of sadness sweeping over me.
Dr Carewell:	We always feel sad when we leave something behind us, Mandy.
Mandy:	*(starts crying again)*
Dr Carewell:	A lot of complicated feelings were tied up in your relationship with Terry. I think we've seen that many of those feelings were pretty self-destructive, but nonetheless they formed an important part of your identity. What I would suggest you are doing now is grieving for a past self, a self which you now see is not conducive to your happiness, but all the same, it hurts.
Mandy:	But I don't feel as if I've left it behind. I feel as if he's left *me* behind!
Dr Carewell:	I may be wrong, but I don't believe you would be crying so freely if you were still holding on to the experience.
Mandy:	There wouldn't really be any point in holding on, would there? There could never be any future for it.
Dr Carewell:	The unconscious mind doesn't always act on reason.
Mandy:	*(snuffling into her tissue)* I bet Mike's a real creep.
Dr Carewell:	*(laughs faintly)*

Mandy:	*(silence)*
Dr Carewell:	*(silence)*
Mandy:	Guess I better say something, eh?
Dr Carewell:	*(silence)*
Mandy:	Now, let's see. How about: The moon's a balloon.
Dr Carewell:	What does a balloon represent to you, Mandy?
Mandy:	Well, it's something that you blow up and then you prick it with a pin and it goes pop.
Dr Carewell:	Do you feel that's what Terry has done to you? Blown you up, pricked you and made you go pop? Is that what Terry has done to your moon?
Mandy:	This is ridiculous.
Dr Carewell:	I'm not so sure it is, Mandy. The moon has always been considered a symbol of femininity. We have learned quite a bit about your masochistic fantasies of the male phallus and your use of the word 'prick' couldn't be more precise.
Mandy:	What about the 'pop' then?
Dr Carewell:	That's the way you felt after being penetrated. Shattered. Rent asunder. Torn apart.
Mandy:	BUT I DIDN'T FEEL THAT.
Dr Carewell:	Your unconscious tells us otherwise, Mandy.
Mandy:	*(screaming)* WHY DO YOU TWIST EVERYTHING I SAY? IT WAS JUST A STUPID PHRASE THAT CAME INTO MY HEAD. THAT'S ALL.
Dr Carewell:	Mandy, as you have seen in the past, it's often these 'stupid phrases', as you call them, that tell us the truth.
Mandy:	*(bursts into hysterical crying)* Oh God, I'm so confused. I don't know any more what I think. Help me. Somebody please help me.

*

As Mandy's analysis continued, she became more involved with Carol and gradually talked less about Terry. This suggested that the analysis was working successfully. After another year Dr Carewell concluded that Mandy was cured and the analysis was terminated.

Mandy and Carol were married and they bought a beautiful home.

They had two children, Sophie and Mary, and both women had successful jobs in banking.

Five years after their marriage, Mandy met Terry in the street one day. He was living in a heterosexual commune and campaigning for rights for straights. Mandy discovered that she was still deeply attracted to him but she could not bring herself to leave her children and the security which the marriage with Carol and the job in the bank represented. She and Terry tried to stay apart but it was impossible.

In the end she settled for a double life: respectable family woman with Carol, Sophie and Mary in Chelsea, on the one hand; hours of furtive merry love with Terry in Hackney, on the other.

The Porn Industry providing
a Useful Social Service

AIDS and...

Pete Freer

[Editor's note: This essay was completed in April 1986 and predates the government campaign. It does not address the issues raised by such a campaign although its central concern is with the strategies we create for ourselves in response to the cultural presentation of AIDS at the time of writing.]

AIDS is, in so many ways, unspeakable: lending itself, like cancer, to whispers from the respectable. Shouted out: 'Fucking AIDS Carrier' has replaced 'Fucking Queer' as the most vulgar and abusive of name callings.

This essay doesn't try to distance itself from its subject. I am not distant from it but subject to the collision of elements implicit within the initials AIDS. Those elements include it being a disease with no cure, unsure diagnostics, forms of transmission centrally connected with sexual contact, with the transfer of blood and in Britain and the US a fatal assumption of belonging to the homosexual population.

The way that we understand sexuality, both our own and other's, is increasingly being mediated by the AIDS crisis. However that crisis and our understandings of it are mediated by theories of sexuality that have existed within common sense. I use this term as Antonio Gramsci[1] uses it, common sense as clusters of concepts, ways of thinking that may or may not be coherent, that remain from past philosophies and religions, from other ways of life.

The relationship between common sense and media representations (defined as widely as possible) is dialectical and reciprocal; i.e. in terms of reciprocity there are moments of active construction occurring between the represented and common sense: they feed each other. Yet there is not a simple correspondence, effects of representations cannot be simply drawn from the nature of those representations. Rather, there are utilisations of those representations that may bear no relation to the intention of the producers.

Such representations are negotiated, utilised and reproduced, often in re-expressive form, by the popular culture and identity to which they refer. However, the element of negotiation is that of struggle defined as collective forms of resistance. Collective here refers to the coming into being of an identity that may not be utterly self-conscious or may even be actively rejected by the subject but involves forms of self-recognition. Recognising ourselves within what is spoken, seen, heard from the larger discourses of society (in its high, official, popular and oppositional forms) as well as in the resistances of the micro discourses of friendships, networks of desire, graffiti of seeming inconsequence.

Forms of language that distance, like: 'forms of transmission that are connected centrally with sexual contact and the transfer of blood', hide the reality that in some parts of the US whole friendship networks are being wiped out. In London there is a feeling of vulnerability that such will become our reality.

'One friend stressed it was like a mini-holocaust, finding whole friendship networks wiped out by death has few parallels except in war.'[2]

He was talking about the US, the situation in Britain is different. But the analogy with war is apt; in a war it is hard not to speak in polemic.

If we don't speak in polemic, what do we speak in? The matter of the thing is those parts of our lives that we speak of in the codings of words like 'sexuality'. A word that hides clusters of concepts and feelings such as love, lust, desire; can evoke loss, regret, loneliness, yet is burdened with the responsibility for our happiness/unhappiness. A word which attempts to divest itself of the mysteries implicit in the clusters of concepts which it stands in for today constantly re-articulated and realigned. A word which, in a sense, reveals some of its meanings through the little stories of touchings, meetings and livings.

A full smile, glorious, he laughs. 'Well, I'm going to die anyway.' 'You're not,' I say, 'it's not inevitable, sex doesn't have to transmit AIDS.' Lost for words we stumble on, having sex that is safe. The satisfactions of it are more in the excitement of the dangers of meeting.

How hard it is to say, but each meeting, each speaking, each touching, constructs the present. How can I re-present my own experience for this essay? My experiences are tied up, like anyone else's, with other people's whose lives, partly understood by others and by me, are not grist to the academic mill.

When we try to account experience we recount memories, we re-present fragments.

1982: The press was full of stories of a mass murder of young (mainly gay) men. Walking on Kilburn High Road with a friend, he said, looking at a newspaper hoarding, 'Things can only get worse.' We had read, but not fully taken in, news of a disease in New York that was killing gay men. We wanted to believe it was a media conspiracy, a lie, yet we had read about it from gay sources we trusted. 'This will change everything,' he said.
1985: I sit in a South London crematorium chapel among people I've known a long time. People from the gay movement, gay liberation, gay theatre; people who have not been afraid to touch whilst being scared

shitless. Friends mourning one of our deaths. No words spoken in this ceremony only the music of strings and small bunches of flowers. A dignity that is daily challenged by those 'gay plague' stories.

1971: Holland Park. I arrive early because so stoned in those days I'd forgotten the route of the parade, remembering only the destination. I think I fell asleep or into a daze on the grass. At any rate my memory recalls the moment of consciousness being the banging of a drum. Eyes open seeing the rich, gaudy colours, rainbows of cloth, long hair flowing across men's and women's shoulders. A predominance of lavender, pink and purple. A voice soars: 'Limp wristed, mincing, lisping, screaming nancy boys.' And a refrain from the crowd: 'Right on.' It is a 'Gay Day' with the Gay Liberation Front Street Theatre. A woman in a bridal gown smeared in blood and vomit is being dragged screaming by mother and sisters; a man in a top hat and tails is also being forced along as he weeps by father and brothers; a priest beckons the wedding party into the Rose Garden. A sinister Victorian perambulator is being pushed by a demonic-looking nanny with a beard. I walk over and look into the pram. My stomach nearly gives way with the sight of the raw flesh and blood in there. The nanny sees my face and smiles kindly. I turn and see a young man in a leotard, broad shouldered, slim, the muscles on his body rendered harmless by the beauty of his face.

What form do these memories take? Stories, pictures, representations that construct within the obviously available ways of saying, me the writer, you the reader, in a relation to being gay. There are the stories we tell ourselves and those we are told; they are not always totally at odds.

The stories continue:

Peter, for that is the name of the man in the leotard, by 1980 was living in New York; no, he isn't dead, he works for the Gay Men's Health Crisis Center as a befriender of isolated gay men with AIDS.

Neither am I dead, many other gay men are: one friend, a founder member of Gay Sweatshop Theatre Company, was found stabbed to death...Priests were allowed to say their prayers (the language of religion taking over when all else fails). Police notices were put up in the arts centre where I work: 'Did you know this man' a 'well known homosexual?' (another language). Of course we fucking did! And, of course, it goes without saying that they never caught the killer.

A few weeks ago at home with the friends I live with, someone said 'Of course, there are far more suicides of gay men than deaths through AIDS.' 'Yes,' we sighed.

The reasonable choice for those who could no longer stand the narrative has always been there.

This is not an attempt to write about dying. Death, a word which has all those meanings from 'coming to terms with it' through to 'oh my dear, but I nearly died'. From the fatalism of religiosity to camp.

1985: Sitting in a pub after a long day at the arts centre. It's a spring evening. The group of young performers I sit with have just finished the first night of a show we've been devising for months. There's a new person with us, Richard, who has been coming to the centre for a couple of weeks. Lively, aggravating, pretty, fourteen and holding forth about everything, particularly sex. I decide to reply to a rhetorical question that assumes my heterosexual complicity with, 'Richard, actually I'm gay.' Disbelief. 'No you're not, you can't be.' 'Why not?' I ask. He can't answer beyond saying 'but, but...' 'Ask anyone,' I say, pointing to the rest of the table engrossed in their conversations. He does so and they say, 'Of course he is.' But Richard suspects me of nodding at them to answer the affirmative and still doesn't believe me. I say, 'Go ask Calvin, he's on the other side of the pub.' So off he goes returning with a laughing Calvin, finally believing me. After Calvin (who isn't gay) and I have exchanged amazement about the difficulty of persuading Richard I am gay, and Calvin has left, a silence descends for a moment. Then a very serious Richard looks directly at me and earnestly asks: 'But, aren't you afraid of dying?'

*

AIDS and the Body of Knowledge

> 'Hold back the edges of your gowns....we are
> going through hell.'[3]

Rock Hudson is dead. So are many others! Another fear eats the soul of the sexual even as it tries to define itself. Any disease represented as incurable is bound to cause panic. However, there seems to be confusion between the panic about Acquired Immune Deficiency Syndrome (AIDS) and the panic around male sexuality in its homosexual forms.

AIDS, interpreted in the languages of politics and culture, has fed into the splitting off of homosex from heterosex. Heterosexuality is already constructed by the massive absence or displacement of homosexual desire: The use of AIDS has been to further isolate the identity 'gay' and limit the domain of the sexual to heterosexuality.

A past moment, sometimes a golden age, of unrestricted sexual freedom is being constructed by gay people. On the one hand its passing is welcomed and a new era of romance and deep friendship envisioned – as if homosexuals had never been friendly or romantic! On the other hand there is a disorientating sense of loss that an unproblematised economy of bodies has not been allowed to continue its tantalising exchanges.

This essay on AIDS only aims to cover limited ground:[4] a terrain inherited from and constructed by past struggles to contain and liberate the sexual.[5] In the metaphor of the terrain there stands a first and last, often lonely, barricade: The Body, the sexualised body which the individual and the communities of interest (informal and formal) will have to defend. This essay is about some elements that structure thoughts which circumscribe those public and private choices that provide a framework of strategy. What I try and do is go behind both my own panic and the media stories to what we might call a repertoire of culturally available knowledges which feeds both. That is, informs the stories on the one hand and makes them effective on the other, fuels the queer-bashers and fractures the dreams of a still emerging social identity, still in the process of becoming, that is larger than the term 'gay community' suggests.

The inter-relation between the social identity 'gay person' and what we call the 'gay community' is a complex one. The latter is not simply the collective term for groups of homosexuals. Gay community is itself a new way of thinking about and organising the gay identity. It is a term that takes in both informal networks and organised groupings politically constituted around defensive, caring, health and informative strategies. There is, of course, a slide or overlap between the informal and formal groupings. There is also a slide between both of these and the commercially constituted provisions like clubs, pubs, magazines, saunas etc. When we talk about gay community it can mean any or all of the above. The origins of gay community are in the 'homosexual underground' or plain 'underground' (with its metaphors of both movement, the wartime resistance, hiddenness and sewage). In the 1950s and before it could be found in every city in Britain.[6] The identity that corresponded to that collectivity was 'homosexual' or 'queer'. Facets and traces of both remain as an inheritance for gay people and others, articulated particularly by the popular press.

The transformation and recomposition of both the individual identity and the collectivity is a complex, unfinished and ongoing history. However we can isolate two conjunctures; firstly, the passing of the 1967 'Sexual Offences Act' and secondly, the formation of a radical popular movement: the Gay Liberation Front (GLF). The Act itself and the struggle to get the state to enact it articulated the idea that if the private sexual doings of people were criminalised they became subject to the worse evil of blackmail. Therefore although openness was definitely not an aim of the Act, it was an inevitable consequence. GLF took that further and declared openness as prerequisite of liberation. 'Coming out' was first an individual act of salvation without which the individual was locked into a secret and neurotic existence. It was also the prerequisite for building a community that was in opposition to the underground's prior secrecy.

In terms of this essay the concept gay community is important in that it constitutes subjects: gay people. That is, those people who see themselves as part of that community, who 'recognise' themselves in the term 'gay'. It also constitutes our main defensive strategies in relation to AIDS. It would be wrong to suppose that everyone who has homosexual sex makes that act of recognition. Homoerotic thoughts or acts do not constitute the subject gay. Nor are subjects unproblematically constituted. We are all subject to multiple discourses whether as women or men, as of a certain class, race, generation, location etc. The identity gay as a subjective experience may be actively rejected or negotiated, especially when articulated as pejorative, dangerous and unrespectable.

In order to think about the relationship between sexuality and disease I want to take on Gramsci's way of thinking about the personality as being:

> strangely composite: it contains Stone Age elements and principles of a more advanced science, prejudices from all past phases of history at the local level and intuitions of a future philosophy which will be that of a human race united the world over.[7]

What Gramsci asks us to come to grips with is that we are products of the historical processes to date which have deposited in us an 'infinity of traces, without leaving an inventory'.

'Traces' that become organised into systems of knowledges and discourses that are spoken and acted upon. However, that does not happen in a simple or linear way: contradiction and irrationality are unadmitted hallmarks of common-sense knowledges or ways of seeing. They are made up from clusters of associations remaining from 'all past phases of history' selected through both conscious and unconscious processes, selectively re-formed and re-framed at the level of both the popular and the official.

I want to look at some of those 'past phases' and their 'traces' which concern the prejudicial and the intuitively progressive. Focusing on ways disease and sexuality are separately and jointly articulated.

The articulations of knowledges are about, among other things, the body. It is intervened in and recomposed in the ways we think of it and live it. Gender-specific knowings attach themselves to it. In the first half of the nineteenth century it was the working-class female body in prostitution which threatened with disease the male forms of both the armed services and the bourgeoisie. Reworkings by the Social Purity Movement produced an overlaying dominant conception of the male as polluter. The body of the homosexual has been constructed as special and different by the discourses of medicine and sexology. Gay people have re-articulated that specialness as a mode of resistance in campness, often being seen and seeing ourselves as a third sex (the 'feminine' man and the 'masculine' woman meeting in discursive constructions).

The discourses of practices of relative openness in the 1960s and 70s meant diversity and ambiguity was layered upon pre-existing ways of seeing, yet always signs, and therefore significations, were generated by the public homosexual body represented and representing itself: those significations articulated beyond the acts of sex.

Articulations formed out of and gaining resonance through memories and half memories; the forgotten but available condensations and displacements of sexual uncertainties into dreams and nightmares. The representations of those traces in images and texts. The infant in the adult. The articulations of law: sentences of time to be spent under a regime of violence for illicit liasons of men in public and private spaces. The face of the prostitute, the rent boy, in the 'truthful' photograph in the paper. The classification of types.

The panics about sexual behaviour of children, young people, women, the disabled, men: of any sexual expression that cuts across the deep structures of race, class or generation. Memories of past crises and panics. Formed and re-formed as coherent narratives and incoherent traces, in which desire is structured along the continuum between pleasure and danger,[8] cross-cut by the continuum between the infant and the adult, in which the individual, as body and mind, remembers: social memories of the self and others. Bodies. The body. Narratives of experience dipping in and out of coherence and consciousness.

On what tracks is this conscious/unconscious running? I think we can isolate two ambiguous but potent themes that inform and structure; these are the concepts of 'nature' and 'disease'. The first links the individual and the material world and is articulated as both the placement and displacement of sexuality and gender onto the concept of nature: 'It's nature; it's only natural.'

Onto the word nature[9] is placed a complexity of often conflicting meanings and concepts, differing ideological positions from different periods of history. Raymond Williams isolates three separate but overlapping meanings from different periods.[10] Firstly from the thirteenth century, nature refers to the essential character of something. Secondly from the fourteenth century, nature is the inherent force which directs the world and/or human beings. Thirdly from the seventeenth century, the material world constituted as having discoverable laws: natural laws. Nature being introduced as a validating concept for law. The word is interesting because of the slide between separate meanings hanging over from different periods. Although confusing, the word still has the power to frame the debates about sexual behaviour in a 'natural light'. Varieties of sexual acts, and the variations in the ways of being a man or a woman (the 'feminine' man and the 'masculine' woman) are articulated as unnatural.[11] Yet we often turn to nature to validate those acts or ways of being: 'It happens in nature, it's only natural!'

The third of the meanings brings nature together with law. It is the vicious and ideological construction called 'survival of the fittest' predicated on the notion of 'natural selection' which comes into being at the end of the nineteenth century. It is concurrent with the classification of types 'in nature' which was being made by doctors, law makers and the emergent sexologists.

We have, therefore, a composite set of seemingly 'natural' sexual tracks. 'Nature' dictates gender roles and heterosexual essentiality. In which the natural is tied to reproduction: essential sexuality is predicated on the production of children; they are the validation of the sexual union; pleasure is only stripped of guilt in the moment of that production. The dominant construct is that the 'natural' force of the sexual is also the driving force. One governed by laws which, even if not subject to legal penalty, will bring 'nature's wrath'.

'Nature's wrath', in this way of thinking, is disease. This is the second and interrelated theme. Disease is the price and punishment for going against 'nature' and the natural laws which justify the dominant and official culture that is also the culture of the church and state. The breakdown of 'nature' is, of course, a 'natural' thing. It is articulated as degeneracy, perversity, withering, wasting, dissolution. Disease as the opposition to 'nature', the opposition to health. And implicated in disease are those who mediate it: the medical profession who historically have delineated and defined, especially in that late nineteenth-century moment of classification of types, what and who was/is well and not so well.

The consolidation of the medical profession ran concurrent to, and was implicated in, the increasing classification of sexual behaviour which derived states of being from the doing of things. The criminal law, with its basis in the 'natural' law, started to have the doctors to explain and even perhaps heal the breakdowns of what was now heterosexual 'nature'; to classify was to know; to make deductions about was to create new knowledges of who we are. Those knowledges were to be instrumental at every level of society in locating deviance and for the deviant to recognise him/herself. Sexual acts that had been seen as sinful and wrong were given new status. This new status was that of a sickness which could easily overlap the old ways of seeing without serious contestation; sickness coupled with perversity stand in opposition to health. Health was articulated to the procreative monogamous couple increasingly under the scrutiny of eugenicism.

The common sense that saw deviancy as wrong, against the law, against 'nature', as our century progressed, became saturated with notions of sickness attached to certain types of people. As Jeffrey Weeks points out,[12] by 1963 93 per cent of people in a survey saw homosexuality as a disease requiring treatment. In the struggle to get the law changed in the sixties one of the main arguments put forward was that criminalisation was inappropriate to a sickness. Simple notions of evil were replaced with more complex notions of pathology. Unlike a natural condition sickness can be caught and cured, but it also spreads. As a 1952 *Sunday Pictorial* piece on 'Evil Men' put it, it was like a 'spreading fungus'. (Many, unhappy with the notion of sickness, posed an alternative hypothesis, that of a condition outside the religious paradigms of good and evil but predicated on and in nature.)

The preoccupation with spies and their sexual doings that has been constant since the 1939-45 war provided a correlation with treason and 'the enemy within',[13] a generic term to cover any group not incorporated into the ways of doing and the ways of seeing of official culture. A culture whose sexual imagination 'was haunted by visions of the slender figure in sweater and tight jeans who lurks in the shadow by the wall, just outside the circle of the lamplight, whisks down the steps of the tube station lavatory, and with a backward glance under the long lashes offers both pleasure and danger'.[14]

A folk devil who at one moment can be a black youth, at another a striking miner, lesbian mother, football supporter, in this case a gay man. As Stuart Hall put it, we place on the folk devil 'all our most intense feelings about things going wrong, and all our fears about what might undermine our fragile securities are projected...as a sort of alter ego for Virtue. In one sense, the folk devil comes up at us unexpectedly, out of the darkness, out of nowhere. In another he is all too familiar; we know him already before he appears. He is the reverse image, the alternative to all we know: the Negation.'[15]

People with AIDS are represented by the official culture as victims and their own executioners.[16] Having (unless not gay and therefore implicitly, and sometimes explicitly, been killed by homosexuality) forfeited their right to public sympathy, they're lucky to get pity. They have become the Negation of the Natural, the heterosexual, the family, by having a different way of being outside the remaining traces of the christian tradition. For which the law-giving god is the final fatherly arbiter of nature. As Donna Summer put it,'AIDS has been sent by God to punish homosexuals.'[17] A statement with a curiously antiquated ring to it, which brings to mind Marx's remark: 'The tradition of the dead generations weighs like a nightmare on the minds of the living.'[18]

These are the images of the nightmare, unnaturalness and sickness personified in the folk devil, the monster, called up by the block headlines 'GAY PLAGUE', and the photographs of suffering, guaranteed as truth by their grainy black and white social-documentary style. Disease itself is news, as with Legionnaire's disease; narratives constructed in the press and on TV reach climaxes and anti-climaxes in the way that news is made to do. There are real pleasures for the recipients of news narratives; it is a genre of entertainment in its own right as much as serials, soap operas or horror movies.

The pleasures are partially voyeuristic in the looking into something that is 'other' from oneself (isn't there always ambivalence in relation to the 'other'?); the titillating/safe pleasure-in-danger[19] is unavailable in the same way to significant groups of people who are either constructed as the problem, or at risk like blood-product users.

I know that the desperate searches for information that my friends and I made had no pleasure in them; we read or watched reports that seemed to gloat at their own 'natural' connection between homosexuality and disease. They either said it straight like Donna Summer or obliquely like the *Daily Mirror*,[20] who had to lie to their 'straight' readers in order to reassure them that heterosexual sex would 'not usually' facilitate the passing of AIDS. No such reassurance was offered to gay men by this the most sympathetic of the popular press.

The formal press and TV channels of communication which pose the problem of AIDS, not as one of public health, but as the problem of the homosexual, have the effectivity of keying into the informal channels that are composed, as Hall puts it, by the 'interplay of knowledges, rumours, folklore and opinions which constitute a critical and primary level at which opinion begins to shape.'[21] Though it is important to note that there is not one unitary 'opinion' but rather sets of opinion that are homogenised in the moment of those opinions being returned to us by the media, and other forms, or utilised to legitimate state policy or lack of it.

We must note that the formal channels are not presenting only one view of either AIDS or gays. Within the institutions of the media there are contestations/pluralities that produce a range of representations; from socio-medical documentaries (with implicit medicalisation of [homo]sexuality), through to Bernard Manning's overreaching homophobia (and just how *is* his crudity received?), to *Eastenders*:

> 'They had better declare the bogs a bender-free zone.'
> 'You can't catch AIDS off toilet seats.'
> ' Fear only comes from ignorance. Gays are just people

with a bigger cross to bear. Live and let live, that's what I say.'[22]

Somewhere in that plurality are the access programmes *Bright Eyes* and *A Plague on You* which try in their allocated time to reverse the direction of the debates.

Also, the notion of a 'negative' representation is difficult precisely because the meanings are not fixed within the text but generated between text and audience. Hence my memories of certain films (e.g. *A Taste of Honey*) that I saw when young, in which the very existence of a gay character was a positive experience – I recognised myself. The same film, seen today, fills me with horror. Now I know I'm not alone; then I didn't.

Secondly, even a 'negative' representation is 'read' through experiences of other texts (inter-textuality), politics, popular movements/cultures, which may alter radically the way they are perceived; e.g. Bernard Manning. The popular press's somewhat sarcastic commentary on his call for all homosexuals to be thrown out of show biz was somewhat at odds with their AIDS articles. As he is someone who trades off racism and sexism does he/it actually amount to much more than a desperate comic in the eyes of the reader and viewer?

For Gramsci, popular culture, which Hall defines by the cluster 'knowledges, rumour, folklore', also contained the 'good sense' of common sense – the live and let live and empathy represented in the *Eastenders* quotes. Representations do also become re-expressed argot and as expressive forms are renegotiated within social situations (think of the 'did you see on telly last night...' conversations). We must remember that readings of news programmes are highly negotiated, ambivalent, even oppositional.

One young woman, who isn't gay, during a discussion of AIDS at the arts centre said that she didn't think AIDS was a problem because 'after all you don't believe anything the papers say about gays'.

However we must still say that there are particular reverberations from the representational forms that relate to sexuality. The repertoire of culturally available 'knowledge, rumours, folklore and opinions' contains the historically specific concepts of nature and sickness: there are traces of the long discredited 'miasma theory' of public health, that saw disease emanating from the ground, or blown in on an ill wind. Pollution slides into moral pollution as Dirk Bogarde dies in Venice[23] for flirting with a thirteen-year-old boy; so policing in 'art' the boundaries of the permissive moment of the sixties. Publicly remembered deaths, a real Oscar Wilde and a fictional Giovanni[24] are part of the available knowledges: the regularity of the natural correlation: the reported 'indecent act', 'taken to court', and the grim word 'suicide' in the national or local paper. Remembered are the past panics and their re-presentation as entertainments, like *Another Country*[25] where treachery is the natural outcome of homosexuality; memories of other court cases where a murderer's successful mitigating circumstance was that his victim was gay; the notion of contagion in the film *Cruising*[26] where Al Pacino becomes infected by homosexuality so that he becomes a murder. Yes, it doesn't make sense, it doesn't have to, once the spectre of sickness rises up a narrative can do anything: become incoherent or enter the world of mythical horror. The vampires walk in the dark night, reproducing and spreading themselves in delicious moments of blood sucking. The real stuff of horror movies and the real stuff of the popular press's medical reports are the real stuff of fear.

Fear that it takes a radical community of homosexuals to start to overcome. Fear, a component of common sense, that it takes everyone to overcome. Fear of being homosexual, because common sense – as popular theory – tells us, echoed in films like *Boys in the Band*: 'Show me a happy homosexual and I'll show you a gay corpse.'[27] Fears distilled into jokes: 'What does AIDS stand for? Answer, asshole injected death sentence'; or 'What does GAY stand for? Answer, got aids yet'; in which our word *gay* that we fought for is turned against us. The sickness is seen as an inevitable consequence of being that which is spoken of by names derived from sexual activities: benders, bum-boys, and brown-hatters. Words are a key component of the repertoires which feed our perceptions of ourselves and others, making it possible or impossible to think of strategies and actions.

We need strategies and actions that run counter to the common-sense panic that constructs the struggled-for gay identity as a threat and wants to prohibit and restrict us for our own good and for the good of others. (An 'us' that does not even incorporate all those who have same-sex sex). For as Foucault points out there are double-sided, counter-productive pleasures inplicit in this, 'pleasures that come of exercising a power that questions, monitors, watches, spies, searches out, palpates, brings to light and on the other the pleasure that kindles at having to evade this power, flee from it, fool it or travesty it'.[28]

Panic and prohibition will not prevent the spread of AIDS, nor make the crisis of gender go away; a crisis that is, as Gramsci says, about the old dying yet the new being unable to be born. The old are the family structures articulated as the norm yet no longer lived, the linking of sexuality to procreation, the subordination of women in that essentialism, the denial of children's and young people's sexualities. Victoria Gillick's action in respect of contraception for young people is the rearguard fight of the old on the offensive; she talks on TV of taking that fight into other areas, and she talks of AIDS in that context. The moral Right will articulate AIDS to their project, co-articulating with those repertoires of fear: the repressed sexuality of the horror movie which is about the exchange of blood, the vampire and contagion; about the normal and good in the narrative, interrupted by the monster.

But there are other articulations that make up different strategies – intimations or 'intuitions of a future philosophy' that Gramsci talks of – the gay organisations struggling to both care and inform: the Terrence Higgins Trust, the gay helplines and the press (see end of essay); the gay community in its organised and informal modes. The really gay films like *The Times of Harvey Milk*[29] that not only show positive images but link them to political and social struggles. Links made by people during the miners' strike; links made by the mining communities who understood, at the height of one of the media panics about both AIDS and themselves, that alliances are more than about getting help, they are about constructing new kinds of common sense, what Gramsci calls 'good sense'.

Good sense that is implicit in the building of links between different groups with the realisation of their differences. The question here is one of collectivities and social identities: the autonomous groups – black people, women, disabled, gay people – produce 'issues' – equal opportunities, age of consent, access, discrimination – that can be safely hived off by both the official culture and the well-meaning Left with the excuse that these are issues which these groups can deal with alone. There is a struggle to keep such 'minority' issues centre stage and not accept the awful responsibility for their own social positioning by the dominant culture: the notion of individual responsibility is one way that society comes to shift its own conflicts onto the minority subject and provides a block to collective and institutional solutions.

AIDS is a social and a medical problem and not a problem of the homosexual or the junkie or any other individual.

That it is seen primarily as a problem of the homosexual led me to write this essay, to try to make sense of why our understandings of AIDS key into both established notions of the sexual and of how a disease is thought and spoken. That we are somehow responsible for our illnesses is, as Susan Sontag says, a 'preposterous and dangerous' view which manages to put the 'onus of the disease on the patient and not only weaken the patient's ability to understand the range of plausible medical treatments but also implicitly direct the patient away from such treatment.'[30] It is as though everyone who wants to do more than hang up the 'closed' sign on the doors of sexual possibility is already a patient: a patient with that responsibility for her or his own condition. The notion of responsibility (complete with its slide into guilt) is at the heart of the safer-sex prescription.

I don't doubt the public health necessity of safer sex! What I doubt is the linking of safer sex with these notions of responsibility rather than notions of pleasure. Ideas of pleasure and responsibility are not the same for different social identities at differing historical moments; for gay men discourses of responsibility have constantly urged us into the status quo's of family, celibacy or a return to the double standard of hidden, furtive and *really* dangerous sex.

Pleasure, it seems to me, is about an expanding universe; responsibility about a limiting one.

What might an expanding universe look like? What representations, venues, spaces and what stories we tell ourselves does it take to bring an expanding universe into focus?

This universe that we experience as the responsibility for AIDS is dumped on us is being struggled over. The notion that celibacy is the only option is still the currency of the Minister of Health and the popular media. In the gay community it is being replaced with the formulation of 'safer sex' or 'playing safe.'[31] If we are to win our own consent to the 'responsible' versions of safer sex then we need to have an expanding universe on our agendas. That is the first step, but deeply implicated in this has to be the wider social agenda.

The 'idea' of AIDS stands in for and signifies a collective loss of nerve about sexuality and pleasure. The popular and respectable press can at last discuss gay sexuality with a censorious vengeance. It is often said that we live in a time when sex is talked about and represented constantly. Yet it seems to me that it is not sex that is talked about so much as the *idea* of sex, an idea that is constantly struggled over. Explicitly putting sexual possibilities on the agendas of institutions concerned with education would be seen to be 'irresponsible' in the present frozen climate. Yet, to continue the metaphor, it is only by unfreezing the possibilities and desires at a wider social level, that at an individual level the regime of safer sex can be set in a context giving it a resonance which makes it a real possibility.

That wider social level is the level of both representations and of the heterosexual. Sexual struggle must be about both dislocating the hetero from the sexual so that a range of possibilities is opened, and dislocating representations of the homosexual trajectory through disease to death: there also being a correspondence with the cultural construction of the sex act as petit mort or 'little death'.

The wider social level is also the level at which heterosexuality is associated with one dominant form of sexuality: penetrative sex. The project to problematise penetrative sex as the zenith of human experience and particularly its place within a total regime of sexuality predates AIDS. Heterosexuals like homosexuals will problematise that model (women have already done so); for the 'plague' which is seen today as being contained within the category 'homosexual' will tomorrow surely be within every category as the disease proliferates. As Susan Sontag put it: 'We are all on the Titanic.'[32]

The forms of responsibility that today are being urged onto gay men will be urged on all: safer sex discourses have articulated pleasure with emphasis on the genitals and the body (dry rubbing) but have stayed within the sex manual approach and an 'it's not so bad really' way of thinking. These discourses assume that the interesting part of 'sexuality' is the sex act, rather than the combination of the sex act with the frissons and anticipations that go with desire. The body provides a multiplicity of sites on which desires can be played out. It is historically specific to our society that the body is constructed as a singularly individual possession; desires may be individual, but they are also social; they involve at least another/'an other', either in fact or in representation. How and where the desires that produce pleasure are to be played out is at the heart of winning consent to safer sex.

There are constraints on public spaces. It has been a continuing project of the police (and therefore of the state) to keep public space clear for the respectable: that public space extends from the parks to Piccadilly Circus, from pub licensing laws to the airwaves, from the frontlines to the magazine and book publishing industry. That project of regulation and control is made possible through cultural and political struggles at the level of the state and relatively autonomous institutions. Those struggles have evoked and constructed notions of the respectable and unrespectable, which at moments in the nineteenth century were attached to the prostitute[33] and the mob[34]; at other moments in our century they are attached to black youth, 'vice' girls or promiscuous homosexuals.

Respectable and unrespectable sexualities correlate with ideas of natural and unnatural, the well and the diseased, as justificatory constructions. Safe but narrowly heterosexual versions of the respectable are posed as the norm in opposition to unrespectable and dangerous sex.

Cutting across these divisions are continuing struggles, by gay people and others, for whom the categories contain degrees of constraint: resisting both the law of the police and the queer-basher (which add an intolerable burden of everyday cruelty to the realities of a disease like AIDS) is not necessarily to change the common sense notion of what 'gay' means. Those essential struggles have to go hand in hand with changing the repertoire of culturally available knowledges about sexuality – i.e. to widen the possibilities so that gay desire is part of common sense understandings of what sexual desire is.

In a book called *The Sexual Outlaw*[35] John Rechy suggested that gay cruising, as outlawry, resisted the control and regulation of sexuality; it was 'revolutionary'. He glorified the idea of the unrespectable and vilified the hypocrisy of the respectable (those grand binary oppositions are always a fertile area). Now the fragility of that glory is evident, yet the project itself, to seek out sites and modes of resistance, is still valid. That is, to seek forms of contact between individuals which will deny the loneliness of that individul possession, which is the body, implicit in the polarity of those grand oppositions.

Keeping the homosexual man off either the literal or metaphoric streets of representation does not pass uncontested. The struggles for gay theatre, film and television, or for the ambivalences of many representations including those of generationally specific fashion and style, continue to create arenas in which sexuality can speak of the possibility of frisson and even maybe bliss...even, and especially, in the face of AIDS.

While the friends, lovers, nurses and doctors of people with AIDS, and the people with AIDS themselves, fight for the dignity and care of life even in the face of death, 'straight' people/heterosexuals must decide quickly where they stand on the terrain of the sexual. This needs to be opened up as a range of desires, not the simple polarities of homo or hetero sexuality. We need more interventions in local government, education, trade unions, the churches etc, to provide the support for people with AIDS and to provide explicit sexual information that can encourage safety but not restrict desire. Also, and dangerously, we need heterosexuals to problematise their own dominance and not leave it only to gay people to put homosexual desire high on the social, cultural and political agenda.

April 1986

Acknowledgements

It is the solidarities of often but not only gay people that make survival and work possible in this and the general crisis...

Thanks to David Aubrey of the British Society For Social Responsibility in Science for inviting me to produce a first draft of this for a seminar in their 1985 series called 'Beneath the White Coat'. Thanks especially to Ken Page and Joyce Canaan of the Centre for Contemporary Cultural Studies (Birmingham), for their repeated and supportive help. Also at CCCS: Richard Johnson, Christine Beasley and Jean Deruz for their critical encouragement. For the enthusiasm of the staff and students of the Birmingham University drama department, who listened to the paper and asked dangerous questions. To Martin Humphries for his helpful editorial work. And finally Martin McCrudden, Robert Hale, Pete Charles and Ray Evans whom I live with, without whom...

Notes

1 Antonio Gramsci, *Prison Notebooks*, especially pp.323-343 'The Study of Philosophy' (London 1971).

2 Kenneth Plummer in *Gay Times*, February 1986.

3 William Carlos Williams. Introduction to Allen Ginsberg's *Howl* for Carl Solomon (San Francisco 1956).

4 For coverage of daily representations in the media see regular articles in *Capital Gay* by Julian Meldrum and others. The gay press has also kept its readers informed of medical developments. See also *Science for the People* 'The Politics of AIDS' Vol. 16 number 5 (Science Resource Centre, 897 Main Street, Cambridge, MA 02139 USA).

5 The terrain of the 'sexual' is constituted by a series of interweaving and co-informing elements. Firstly the institutions and discourses of culture: from art to advertising, from the novel to soap opera, from high culture to the popular, words and images, narratives and poems. Secondly by the popular movements that define the sexual even as they seek to control and transform it. Informed by thirdly the theories of sexuality from the sexologists through to Reich and Marcuse. Fourthly by the state (with its own use of theory) in its policies and practices also of control, regulation and transformation. The terrain is struggled over. That struggle is a constant war of position. AIDS is being used to challenge the shifts in hegemony effected by the gay movement in coalition with other movements.

6 Tom A. Cullen, 'Homosexuality and British opinion' in *New Republic*, 25 April 1955.

7 Gramsci, op. cit., p.324.

8 Gordon & Dubois, 'Between Pleasure and Danger' in *Feminist Review* 13. This looks at the construction of the nineteenth-century social purity movement in relation to feminism. For a useful introduction to thinking about cross-generational sex see Mica Nava 'Drawing the Line', in *Gender and Generation*, eds McRobbie and Nava (London 1984).

9 See Jon Ward's contribution to this book, 'The Nature of Heterosexuality', for a fuller discussion of the concept of nature.

10 Raymond Williams, *Keywords* (London 1976).

11 The trajectory of essential gender roles dictated by biology in Germany in the thirties led to the systematic imprisonment and killing of homosexuals. See Heinz Heger, *The Men with the Pink Triangle* (GMP 1980).

12 Jeffrey Weeks, *Sex, Politics and Society: the regulation of sexuality since 1800* (London 1981)

13 The term 'the enemy within' has a contemporary ring to it given its use during the miners' strike by Thatcher; however it has an older use in the context of post-1945 spy panics. Such spy panics contain linkages between political dissent and sexuality with cancer being used as a metaphor about the existence of both in society. The 'enemy within' also has the effect of constructing a mythic nation in which the deep antagonisms of class, race and gender disappear.

14 Rebecca West, *The Decline and Fall of Treason*, Chapter 5 (London 1982).

15 Stuart Hall, Chas Critcher, Tony Jefferson, John Clarke and Brian Roberts, *Policing the Crisis: Mugging, the State and Law & Order* (London 1978), and Cohen *Folk Devils and Moral Panics, the Creation of the Mods and Rockers* (London 1972).

16 The notion of 'victim' predominates in official discourses not only in relation to AIDS but to the passivity attributed, often, to subordinate groups. Those discourses are obvious in the popular press and implicit in government and social policy.

17 *Capital Gay* quoting *New York Native* on Donna Summer's comments at Merriville, Indiana, July 1983.

18 Karl Marx, 'The Eighteenth Brumaire of Louis Bonaparte' in *Surveys from Exile* (Harmondsworth 1973).

19 Though the popular press does offer safe 'pleasure-in-danger', nevertheless readers often renegotiate those discourses empathetically.

20 *Daily Mirror*, 5 March 1985. 'AIDS The Truth' was the ironic title to a piece that seemed to have the aim of reassuring heterosexuals that they were safe whilst presenting the gay community as uncaring. No reference was made to the work of the Terrence Higgins Trust or Gay Switchboard.

21 Hall *et al, Policing the Crisis.*

22 *Eastenders*, a BBC-TV soap opera, broadcast 30 January 1986.

23 Film: *Death in Venice*. Director L. Visconti 1971.

24 James Baldwin, *Giovanni's Room* (London 1957).

25 Film: *Another Country*. Director M. Kanievska 1984. Based on the play of the same name by Julian Mitchell.

26 Film: *Cruising*. Director W. Friedkin 1980. Based on the novel of the same name by Gerald Walker (1970).

27 Film: *Boys in the Band*. Director W. Friedkin 1970. Based on the play of the same name by Mart Crowley.

28 M. Foucault, *The History of Sexuality, volume 1 an introduction* (New York 1980).

29 Film: *The Times of Harvey Milk*. Documentary directed by Robert Epstein & Richard Schmiechen 1984.

30 Susan Sontag, *Illness as a Metaphor* (Harmondsworth 1983).

31 Safer sex can be seen as a further contradictory medicalisation of homosexuality in which gay men educate themselves in areas of medicine, both orthodox and alternative. Taking place within discourses of pathologisation. Evidenced by the coalition between gay organisations, individuals and parts of the medical profession which stand between us and another holocaust.

32 Susan Sontag in conversation on *Voices*, Channel 4, 22 May 1985.

33 Judith Walkowitz, *Prostitution and Victorian Society* (Cambridge 1980).

34 Gareth Stedman Jones, *Outcast London* (Oxford 1971).

35 John Rechy, *The Sexual Outlaw* (London 1978).

The Terrence Higgins Trust, BM/AIDS, London WC1N 3XX, runs an AIDS information line on 01-242 1010 from 7pm to 10pm Mondays to Fridays.

London Lesbian and Gay Switchboard, for information about gay social, cultural and political groups, can be contacted on 01-837 7324. They provide a 24-hour service.

And the Moral of These Stories Is...?

Alison Hennegan

Facts come before theories. Facts are hard. 'Hard facts': hard to face, hard to deal with, hard to live with. What follows is a selection of facts, drawn from experience, communicated by anecdote.

I chose these facts, these experiences, these anecdotes because each of them constantly resurfaces in my mind: memories of physical settings, facial expressions, tones of voice, feelings left hanging in the rooms where the incidents happened, present and re-present themselves time and time again.

They do so, I believe, because each in its own way has demonstrated to me with particular force that though homosexuals and heterosexuals may inhabit the same world, we often see and experience it so differently that we remain at least one world apart.

After facts sometimes come theories. Not, in this case, grand system-building ones, just observations, thoughts, conclusions prompted by the incidents recounted here and following them in the text.

*

Five summers ago at an international gay conference I met a man from Central Europe whom I shall call Pavel. He said he had very much wanted to talk to me because people had told him I might be able to help.

At home he had an elderly friend, an eminent writer much honoured in his own and surrounding countries, virtually unknown in the West. Like us, his friend was homosexual. For years he had concealed his sexual orientation and toed the Party line, partly through fear, partly because he had, with good reason, hopes of winning high State distinction for his work. Public declaration of his homosexuality might bring danger, would certainly bring discredit. But now that he was growing older, Pavel told me, he grew impatient and angry at the long years of concealment. He wanted to be able to write directly of the emotions and desire which had been central but submerged in his life. He also wanted to be known and read in the West.

By coincidence a woman friend of mine, herself one of Pavel's compatriots, though long resident in England, greatly admires the writer. She is also a translator. I put her in touch with Pavel who had returned to his home. They corresponded and began successful negotiations to obtain permission for her to translate one of the writer's novels (a novel, by the way, which is a sustained allegory for his desolation when the Jewish boy whom he loved in the 1930s was taken by the Nazis and deported to an unrecorded death in one of the Camps).

Meanwhile I told my friend as much as I could remember of what Pavel had told me about the writer. In particular I tell her about the way in which he believes his homosexuality and the need to keep it secret has affected his choice of subjects and his treatment of them. I tell her of his passionate desire that he could write about it without the safe distancing of allegory and metaphor.

She listens, a little distant, wary, not fully engaged. Am I *sure*, she asks. For I must remember that in Central Europe scandal is an even more powerful political weapon and one more ruthlessly and skilfully used than it is in the West. Like all eminent men, the author has enemies. What better way to discredit him than to spread the rumour that he's queer? But why, I ask, should a man who is his friend, who is working hard on his behalf, spread harmful lies? She remains unconvinced. Later that evening she discusses it with her husband who finds incredible – and therefore dismisses – the very idea that the writer may be homosexual.

Just three years later, the summer before last, my friend pays one of her spasmodic visits. She and her husband have just returned from Munich where, she tells me, they met an old friend who is also a friend of the writer. And do you know what? The writer *is* homosexual. They know it now because their (very heterosexual male) friend has told them so. And, she adds, their friend says the writer is a coward who will risk nothing.

When my friend had left I realised, dimly at first then more clearly and strongly, that I was very, very angry. For three years she hadn't actually believed me. Now she does because a heterosexual man confirmed that I was right.

Homosexuals, apparently, do not exist until a heterosexual says they do. We know that already, I suppose, from the 'proof' of our homosexuality which so many of us were hounded into producing – for doctors, parents, psychiatrists, youth counsellors, friends – before the rest of the world would consent to accept our own statements about our sexuality.

You're homosexual if they say you are.

You aren't until they do.

Moreover, homosexuals – even if they're friends of fifteen years' standing – clearly are not to be trusted to tell the truth about each other. All they do is 'see it everywhere', slander the world in an insane recruiting fury. And if they can't find recruits they invent them. They even smear eminent and esteemed authors in their pathological efforts to raise their own self-esteem by annexing the illustrious. How extremely *unlikely* that a fine writer would be homosexual.

Yet, unfairly, this one was. In which case, how *cowardly* of him not to have told them before! Heads they win, tails we lose. Later that evening as I brood over the day's revelations I find myself wondering why he should ever risk anything ever again for people who, fundamentally, think he's too good to be gay.

★

I am attending the Memorial Service of a woman whom I did not know well enough to call a friend. I am attending partly for myself, because I liked the woman, admired and respected her, felt warmly towards her. But mostly I am attending on behalf of someone whom I know well enough to number amongst my very closest friends and she, thousands of miles away in Canada, cannot be here and so much needs to be because she very much loved the dead woman although they were never lovers.

The woman was only thirty-eight when she died. She was a fine teacher, a fine scholar with an international reputation. She also had a husband and three children. Her husband, in minor orders, takes the service. Every time he speaks it is to wrest the focus from her to him. We hear of *his* emotions at her death, her part in *his* career.

With disbelief I hear him announce that *his* son will read the lesson. My involuntary gasp of shock seems to me to fill the back of the church but no one notices. For the next few minutes I'm hot with fury and hear in my head the endlessly repeated words: 'How dare he? How *dare* he? Couldn't he, just this once, say 'her son' or, if that's too much to ask, couldn't he, even once, say 'our son'? You bastard, you *bastard*!'

Later in the service one of her colleagues, another woman, gives a brief address. She takes as her starting point Montaigne's words about his beloved friend, Etienne de la Boétie:

> If a man urge me to tell wherefore I loved him, I feele it cannot be expressed but by answering: Because it was he, because it was myselfe.

Magnificent words and pleasingly familiar in Florio's Elizabethan translation to this largely academic congregation. They settle themselves comfortably to listen to an elegant albeit moving disquisition from a fellow scholar in which she draws an analogy between Montaigne's feelings for de la Boétie and her own for her dead colleague and friend.

My own feelings are those of outrage. I know that the speaker and the woman of whom she speaks had to juggle the innumerable demands of teaching and research, children and husbands, perform the perennial female balancing trick between two full-time jobs, Home versus Career. They managed it pretty well. Full marks: for trying; for guts; for salvaging as much as they did; for ingeniously carving out small nuggets of time and energy to be given to women friends when – and only when – familial duties are fulfilled. But does the speaker really think such painstaking quarrying can be compared to that passionate intensity which Montaigne felt for Etienne and which so clearly – perhaps cruelly, and perhaps not in an age of arranged marriages – relegated Mme Montaigne to second place?

No, it can't, and for me the attempt to do so is heterosexuality at its old dishonest game: wanting the pleasures of homoerotic love with none of the risks, the fantasy without the hard, unhonoured and socially uncelebrated work which would make it reality.

Moreover I know quite well that the woman who speaks is not comfortable with modern-day declarations of truly passionate love between people of the same sex. Montaigne's words uttered today to a male friend would make her uneasy. I know that when she first learned that my friend now absent in Canada was a lesbian, she dropped her. Unlike the dead woman, who did not keep her beloved Montaigne – and his passionate emotions – safely confined to the sixteenth century but recognised a kinship between Montaigne's love for de la Boétie and my friend's for her, even though she herself was not a lesbian.

For me, the service is redeemed only by the final speaker – a young nun (the dead woman was a Catholic convert although she is being commemorated in an Anglican church). The nun who might have been expected to elevate the achievements of Christian Wife- and Motherhood above all else, recognises them but does not grovel to them. She takes them and weaves them, together with details of the woman's intellectual life and eager spiritual questing, into a picture of someone who knew that her marriage to one man and the bearing of three children did not, should not and could not define the sum of her existence. (Is it, I find myself wondering as her address continues, a coincidence that the only speaker apparently able or inclined to make that point in this company should be a celibate woman religious whose 'marriage' is to be union with an incorporeal godhead?)

Later, via *The Times*, then that bastion of convention, the nun's point is reinforced. The paper publishes an obituary, weeks late because the husband had originally said one was not necessary. The woman colleague who had spoken at the service submits one just the same. It duly appears, half a page deep and three columns wide. It recounts in impressive detail the dead woman's scholarly achievements. Her husband is confined to one line at the end.

★

It is eleven o'clock at night, four and a half years ago. For the fifth time that evening I am telephoning a maternity hospital trying to find out if the woman who for fifteen years has mattered more to me than anyone else has been safely delivered of her first child.

A nurse answers. 'Are you family?' she asks. Too taken aback to answer I am silent. 'Are you *family*?', she repeats irritably.

This time I can answer but am too proud to lie. No, I say. 'Well, you'll have to ask her husband tomorrow, then.' Can she not, I ask, even tell me if my friend is safe? No. She cannot. Only family can be told. I must speak to her husband in the morning. Could she, I ask, possibly take a message to the husband, who I know is with his wife, and ask him to ring me tonight? 'We're very *busy*, you know,' she scolds and hangs up.

I pass a wretched night. It's no good saying nobody dies in childbirth these days. They do – one of my friends and two acquaintances in the last ten years. And I've seen enough statistics for perinatal deaths in Britain. I rehearse them through a night full of nauseous anxiety – anxiety and a steadily mounting anger.

Because I am not 'family', I have to sweat it out, denied vital information made freely available to in-laws some of whom she doesn't even like. Why didn't I take the easy way out, say firmly 'Yes, I'm her sister, Alison'?

Gradually I realise I refused the easy way because it was too difficult. It entailed playing their game, agreeing that only blood ties and marriage certificates give validity to human relationships.

Next morning at work gay friends tell me I was crazy to give myself hours of unnecessary misery when a strong, brazen lie could have brought relief. And anyway, they say, it's a way of getting your own back, isn't it, a way of re-defining their terms for them without their even knowing it. You *are* 'family' because you and she *are* sisters, sisters in sisterhood.

But I remain stubbornly unconvinced. Terms cannot be considered 're-defined' until all parties using them agree about their new meanings. Later that day I learn from her husband, exultant, relieved, eager to share his happiness and include me in it, that their daughter had already completed three hours of triumphantly healthy life when I spoke to the night nurse.

I had assumed that this particular anecdote would need no commentary. Its significance seemed so self-evident to me. But I have discovered that whereas every homosexual person who has heard me tell it has empathised immediately and strongly with the pain it describes, my reasons for including it here are less apparent to them.

For me the incident yields meanings far beyond the initial and fairly obvious point: that membership of a 'family', defined by blood ties and endorsed by official state documents, gives 'rights' and privileges. And gives them regardless of the true state that may exist between members of that unit (dislike, indifference, lack of respect) and regardless of the state that may exist between individuals within the unit and those outside it (love, loyalty, concern).

(Ironically, had my friend been *un*married, there would have been greater flexibility. There has to be: break the first rule – Only The Married May Bear Children – and the rest tend to fall by the wayside. Regulations about visitors, labour partners, next-of-kin, have been far more bendable for unmarried friends who gave birth in a hospital. You can, of course, put it another way, as these days I prefer to do: *unless* you break the first rule, none of the others will be modified. For as long as marriage and childbirth and heterosexuality remain inextricably linked in the official mind, husbands, fathers and families will have their assumed needs met at the expense of others'.)

There are, I believe, other reasons why the incident I've described happened and they are all connected with the fact that I was attempting to deal with a hospital. I remember the evening when my friend told me she had decided to give birth there rather than at home. The reasons seemed reasonable indeed: a first birth at a (comparatively) late age; immediate access to a wider range of medical attention if things went wrong. But notwithstanding I felt a chill.

Few professions offer more vivid examples of sexism constantly at work than modern medicine and few professions have promulgated more deeply cherished myths and stereotypes to conceal the fact. Just think of all those battle-axe matrons and indomitable, bustling ward sisters, who, single-handed, keep at bay whole battalions of cowed consultants and eminent but trembling surgeons. Rigidly starched women whose word is law but whose crisply laundered aprons (invariably) conceal the warmest of hearts.

Maybe. But the stereotypes – and the real life models where they exist – cannot obscure the fact that modern medicine elevates (usually male) doctors and consultants at the expense of (usually female) nurses; that modern medicine has elevated a theory and practice which constantly fails to consider the need of the whole person, rather than the specific illness or complaint; that modern medicine has preferred to consult its own convenience and timetable before the needs of the patient (the inducing of babies, for instance, and the use of drugs which so accelerate the rate of contractions that a woman giving birth cannot pace her breathing or steward her strength and effort effectively); that in the areas of gynaecology and childbirth particularly, modern medicine is the product of a bitter battle waged during the eighteenth and nineteenth centuries in which women – as herbalists, as midwives and as childbearers – were increasingly marginalised, pathologised and ejected. And, finally, that it is modern medicine which has made pregnancy and childbirth a sickness, has declared that children must be born in hospitals. In 1938 and 1948 it was still (comparatively) easy for my mother to say of her approaching confinements: 'The child was conceived in this bed and it's being *born* in this bed. I'm having a *baby*, for heaven's sake, not a disease.' Much harder now for a woman to feel comfortable or safe about making that stand (*pace* Leboyer). Home midwifery is under economic attack and increasingly we hear the insidious argument that it is irresponsible of a woman to refuse a hospital birth, a negation of her duty (to whom or what?).

All these factors and others played a part during my friend's confinement. There *was* a kindly gorgon of a midwife who kept at bay the young (male) doctors who sauntered in now and then during labour, debating whether it was happening 'quickly enough' (quickly enough for whom or what?) and saying nonchalantly that perhaps they'd have to take steps to 'hurry things along a bit' (why?). My friend was, without her knowledge and therefore without her consent, injected with a drug which changed the pace of her labour and therefore interfered with the rhythm which she and her body were working out together.

Later, labour over and the child born, it was a male doctor who sewed her torn flesh, smoking as he did so, and causing her rather more pain than the delivery. (She was at least spared the comment 'There you are, tight as a virgin. Your husband will be pleased!' which another of my friends had to endure.) I asked her later why she hadn't complained. She said 'You can't, you can't make a fuss. They have the upper hand.'

Later still when I visited her I was struck by the way in which (female) nurses and auxiliaries attempted to infantilise the women in their care. They were all 'good girls', 'bad girls', 'naughty girls', 'clever girls'. What was going on here? I asked myself.

Eventually I began to wonder whether the infantilisation sprang from a female nursing staff's deep emotional confusion caused by working – as women, with women, and, supposedly, on behalf of women – under the dominion of a predominantly male profession so deeply inimical to and uncomprehending of the coming of new life. For however intimidated, apprehensive, manipulated or bullied the women might be as patients, in the act of giving birth each was a flagrant, undeniable witness to the uniquely female capacity to bear a new life. How much easier in this male enclave to deny female power by reducing those who demonstrate it to the status of children – good ones, bad ones, naughty ones and clever ones, but all of them subordinate. So, irony of ironies, women who have just given birth to a new child are themselves called children.

And, if we pause for a moment to don our social historians' hats, we may simply observe that at this point, sadly and predictably, today's medical practice takes its place within a centuries-long tradition – drawn from and bolstered by the pronouncements of theologians, philosophers and jurists – which declares that Woman, the Eternal Asinine, is the Child to Man's unimpregnable Adult.

There are other reasons why I think that the sleepless night of sickening anxiety which I sweated my way through four and a half years ago was inextricably linked with heterosexuality. But perhaps I've said enough to be going on with....

INTERLUDE

'So tell me,' urges a friend excitedly, 'what was Adrienne Rich *like*, what did she say?' I look back over my interview with Rich earlier that afternoon and in my mind replay the conversations held and overheard that evening at the party given by her publishers. What to select? The friend and her husband, impatient with eagerness to hear, wait for me to marshall my thoughts.

Well, I say, selecting what made the deepest impressions, there were three things in particular. One was that she's never yet met the heterosexual woman who didn't want to make an honourable exception for *her* man when discussing men's treatment of women. The second was that she'd never yet met the heterosexual man who didn't grow extremely angry at the suggestion that, whether he wanted to or not, he inevitably partook of privileges enjoyed at women's expense. The third was that she'd never yet met the heterosexual man who didn't grow extremely angry at the suggestion that heterosexuality and its attendant emotions were not 'natural' – spontaneous, inevitable, predestined by biology, fate and world order – but institutionalised – carefully inculcated, fostered and enforced by an array of religious, cultural and political sanctions.

The friend's husband grows extremely angry. He is particularly distressed at the notion of heterosexuality as an Institution. A violent row develops.

The friend withdraws herself from the supper table and goes to the sink to wash up. For the duration of the row all I see is her back. Later when I charge her with cowardice and evasion, she says she thinks it's counter-productive to push men, especially those fundamentally well disposed towards feminism, beyond a certain point. What that point is I am unable to discover from her.

Two days later I tell a close gay male friend about the evening. He is quick to empathise, quick to recognise the abundant ironies. That night he recounts the episode to his own male lover who grows extremely angry and accuses him and me, in my absence, of gross over-reaction.

During the next two years daily experience confirms my opinion that Rich is right. Her beliefs on the subject of institutionalised heterosexuality have become my own. I express them one summer afternoon to a comparatively new acquaintance, a young man acting as my proxy-host during a week's visit to a mutual friend. He grows extremely angry and (with what I later come to realise was a most uncharacteristic violation of his personal laws of hospitality) tells me that I'm talking 'absolute rubbish, absolute rot, nonsense!'

Like any other homosexual, I've grown accustomed over the years to the demand that I justify, explain my 'unnatural' self. These days I don't always bother, but I know how to if I must. After all, I've had twenty-five years in which to work out my arguments. Heterosexuals, it seems, once forbidden to play the trump card of their own unquestioned 'naturalness', find explanations harder.

END OF INTERLUDE

It's getting on for midnight. I am with the friend whose first confinement caused me such a welter of untidy emotions. We are working in her now too small flat, in the room which doubles as a study and bedroom for her and her husband. She is copy-editing a manuscript at the desk. I lounge on the bed reading a book whose author I am soon to interview. In the room on the right her new daughter is sleeping. In the room on the left her husband agonises over a script.

We have been working for some hours now, stopping only for her to feed and change the child. She's weary, stiff and just a little bored. Diligently she tries to concentrate but clearly her thoughts are wandering. She stretches mightily, glances at me, slightly conspirato-rially, slightly defiantly as though waiting to see whether I'll be disapproving or delighted that work is, apparently, over for the evening. I laugh at her, she laughs back, says, lapsing into the baby talk of an earlier shared time, 'I'se *bored*!', and reaches for her guitar.

For the next twenty minutes or so she sings the songs she played and sung for me throughout our undergraduate years – bawdy Restoration ballads, whimsical settings of the whimsical Mr Lear, traditional folk songs. But mostly she sings Elizabethan, Jacobean and Caroline love songs, plangent, despairing, railing, yearning songs of lovers 'who never meant to fall in love', who asked angrily 'what then is love but mourning?' And any one of these songs has the power to evoke instantly a shared adolescence and early womanhood in which, ignorant, inexperienced, uncertain and often more than a little scared, she and I took a deep breath and tried to find our way through the minefield of a close friendship between her (loving but heterosexual) and me (lesbian and in love). We managed – more or less.

She sings until the past is everywhere, the room crowded with misunderstandings, reconciliations, tensions, near-rows coldly avoided, desperate struggles after honesty, cowardly retreats from it, pleas for help met immediately and unstintingly, whole evenings of laughter, triggered off by nobody remembers what and erupting again long after we thought we had it under control.

She lays aside the guitar, lights up a cigarette, looks at me and says nothing.

And nothing.

And nothing.

I feel tension mounting in me, feel panic not far away and am unable to speak. She goes on smoking, occasionally looking at me, more often staring into the middle distance. My heart begins to beat uncomfortably fast and I find it difficult to look at her. I want to say something which will affirm my love, so strongly rooted in the past, without endangering the present and future.

I try out phrases in my head and discard them all: too bathetic, too cringing, too sentimental, too melodramatic, too maudlin, too embarrassing. What I really want to say is 'You know I still love you as much as ever, don't you?' But I can find no way of making it a statement rather than a demand. And anyway I've left it too long. The silence has lasted several minutes. Whatever breaks it must be portentous or utterly trivial.

She looks at me, finishes her cigarette, makes a very thorough job of stubbing it out, sighs and says 'Well, that's that, then.' My heart's still galloping, my mouth's dry and although I am quite consciously commanding my lips to open and frame the words, they won't obey.

She comes over and puts the guitar away in its case which lies open at my feet. As she stands in front of me I put my arms around her waist and issuing one last furious command to my craven lips make them say

'I do love you.' 'Yes,' she says, 'I know' and puts her arms around me. We stay like that for some moments but neither of us speaks until she draws away and says 'I'm going to put the kettle on for some tea.' A truly resounding return to everyday life.

But I cannot dislodge the conviction that that evening I was offered an opportunity – for greater truth, greater trust – which my cowardice refused to take. Four years later the episode remains clearly recorded in my memory where I play it back time and again, nagging, teasing, worrying it to yield up its meaning.

Now, it is perfectly possible that none of this ever happened. Oh yes, the songs were sung and silence followed them. *That* happened, certainly. But possibly for her it was an empty silence, a peaceful silence, a silence free from questions pressing to be voiced, fears fretting to be acknowledged. What, if anything, did that silence mean?

I cannot tell because I could not ask. And I could not ask because I could not believe I had the right to. Too many things urged silence, conspired to make me feel ineligible to ask, to know.

The child asleep next door, for example. Her coming changed an affair into a marriage which gave her legitimacy but takes away many of her mother's freedoms and subtly changes the person she can be for her friends. Marriage takes even the surname by which I knew her for twelve years before the child was conceived, gives her a new name which severs continuity with the past and by some curious alchemical reversal declares that past to be a baser metal, devalued, relinquishable.

Originally she and her husband agreed she'd keep her own name. She did so for a while but it created confusion and difficulties with officialdom, GPs, Inland Revenue. For a while she used both names. Gradually she abandoned the earlier one. Now I am the only person who fights a stubborn, pointless rearguard action, angrily determined to use her 'real' name, her true name, the name she had when I first knew her, the only name which denotes the person she is to me.

Stubbornly I go on writing that first name on envelopes, using it when I leave telephone messages for her with colleagues who, like me, first knew her as an unmarried woman. But gradually, as five years pass, the first name conveys nothing. '*Who?*', say the colleagues by now so accustomed to her married name that the first is meaningless, describes a non-existent person.

The woman it referred to might as well be dead. And so, in one sense, she is because the relationship which existed between herself, her name and those who knew her by it, was quite formally terminated by a marriage contracted largely to ensure that her unborn daughter should have the legal right to bear her father's name, should be spared any penalty which her mother's might bring.

Sometimes I tell myself I'm foolish to mind so much, petty, stupid, childish. She was, presumably, happy to take her husband's name. For her, clearly, no sense of self resides in the one she relinquished so easily. It wasn't, in the end, important enough to keep.

Yet for me the change is a constant source of pain, anger and incomprehension. Identity is fragile enough, God knows. How, I constantly ask myself, can any woman be so sure of it, so careless of it, that she willingly changes the name which first connoted it, willingly blends, blurs, merges and loses it in a male other's – in *any* other's?

Abandoning the name so lightly represents to me an abandonment and desertion of the past in which she bore it. As part of that past I feel abandoned too. For me the present which we continue to share is weakened, the future made more perilous.

When I talk like this to women friends I notice it is the lesbians among them who understand what I am saying, what I am feeling. The others seem not to. I am forced back upon the conclusion that one of the things that marks and makes a lesbian is a fundamental determination to safeguard the constantly assaulted sense of self, coupled with the recognition that for the female self, union with the male must mean her obliteration if 'union' entails seeking public and state endorsement of what are supposedly 'private' sexual and emotional arrangements.

The child asleep next door did not cause her mother's willingness to snap the thread of continuity represented by her first name. Her coming simply precipitated it, made it manifest. But it is the assumption of the name, not the birth of the child or even the marriage itself, which says more clearly to me than anything else that her mother has now fully assumed the role of Married Woman, has agreed to be denoted by and obedient to a definition which carries with it so many powerful messages.

And all of them warn me off, exclude me, tell me there are things I have no right to say, to ask, to feel. However much my reason may rebel against the implicit *dictat*, however cogent and witty may be my intellect's dissection of marriage as historical phenomenon and cultural institution, my emotions keep me firmly censored. Reason rebels but old learned responses assert that she is 'his', that in their emotional lives married people are accountable to no one but themselves, that marriage is entitled to expunge the claims of earlier ties.

And many married women in their turn, I believe, feel bound by and anxious for the safety of those same censored emotions. They feel obliged not to wonder, not to wander – even in their thoughts – outside that defining role of 'married woman', especially not if their wanderings bring them dangerously close to the Border which separates the fundamentally warring countries of Heterosexuality and Homosexuality.

There is additional reason for my cowardice, I have come to believe.

On the whole I have had an easy time of it as a lesbian. My parents didn't hustle me off to be cured by the GP, psychoanalysed by the shrink, made to see the error of my ways by a priest. I lost no jobs because of my publicly acknowledged sexuality. It even gained me one – and a marvellous one at that – which gave me almost six years of features work and literary journalism for the original *Gay News*. I've not been evicted by landlords, ostracised by neighbours, hounded by the police, beaten up by marauding yobboes looking for a lezzie to bash (though I've had three uncomfortably narrow escapes).

Like most gay people I number amongst my friends women and men who have suffered all the above, and more. But for me it's been, as it were, 'an easy lesbianism', rather in the way that doctors refer to 'an easy birth' or 'an easy death'. 'Easy', that is, in relation to what other poor wretches must endure. I have, it seems, come through. But not, I often realise now, unscathed, unscarred.

Buried so deep that it's taken me years to recognise it is the assumption that in a friendship with a heterosexual woman my own emotional needs must be subordinated to hers, that she is 'entitled' to be spared the pain and conflict which may arise when the values of her heterosexual world collide with those of my lesbian one.

I find myself condoning behaviour which I woud not tolerate for a moment in lesbian friends. I find myself accepting remnants of time, energy and thought, find myself accepting (albeit mutinously) that the claims of husbands and children must and should always come first.

Of my lesbian friends who live in close relationships with one sexual partner and who have young children, none of them expects or wants allowances of that sort to be made. On the rare occasions when conflicting claims force them to answer the needs of a lover rather than friend, their feelings are those of unhappiness at an unsatisfactory outcome rather than confidence in a social duty rightly done. The freedom I feel to call on their friendship, the demands I feel able to make on it are qualitatively different from those I feel able to make on that of my heterosexual women friends whose lives are permanently linked with men. Whilst railing internally against the fact that women whom I love constantly give to men the central place in their lives, I do not feel entitled to make my dissatisfaction, my anger, overt, explicit, unmistakable.

I think there can, in the end, be only one explanation for that. I think it must mean that at an absolutely basic level, somewhere beyond rationality, I believe that I as a woman, and a lesbian woman, am rightly less important than any man could be.

My reason repudiates it fiercely, as do my politics, my feminism, and my sense of justice. Nevertheless, there, deeply buried, always waiting to catch me out, trip me up, undermine me, is that lurking potent response.

I fight it, of course. Perhaps in the end I'll conquer it. Meanwhile it remains, Heterosexuality's fiendish little landmine, just waiting for those moments when....

A Potential Mandarin having his Priorities Straightened Out

Choosing with Care:
working with non-gay men

Martin Humphries

Most of us have some connexions with the heterosexual world. These can be as minimal as when shopping or travelling but often the connexion is through work of one sort or another. Unlike our social lives we do not, at times, seem to have much choice about the work we do. But there are occasions when we do choose who to work with. In this essay i want to talk about my experience of working with non-gay men in a political situation. This is not in any way unique, our ways of working within the heterosexual world are diverse. We may work in the peace movement, the Labour Party, school, college, office, factory or any combination of these. Our gayness may be explicit or hidden depending on our relationship to those we work with. My clearly defined working relationships with heterosexuals have been within my housing cooperative; at the arts and community centre where i was a paid worker for four years; and as a member of the Achilles Heel Collective. It is my experience with Achilles Heel and the issues it raises that i wish to focus on here.

First Contacts

Achilles Heel is a profeminist, anti-sexist writing and publishing collective committed to supporting men writing about sexual politics and socialism. Most of the work appeared in a journal of the same name which was first publshed in 1978. In this context i was a gay man working with profeminist men, some of whom had relationships with men but who did not clearly define themselves as gay, to produce a journal of anti-sexist (men's) politics. I joined the collective in 1979 with a hazy idea that a way forward was through building and establishing political alliances with non-gay men who were committed to sexual politics. At that time i was politically untutored – how 'tutored' i am now is open to debate. I had a personal awareness of the oppression of gay men and felt that feminism aligned with socialism was a concrete way of changing the world. My political his-story, in terms of learning and understanding theory, was only just beginning. I was searching for ways to develop.

My involvement in Achilles Heel resulted from reading the first issue published in the summer of 1978. Then i was coming out more strongly as a gay man, recovering from the breakdown of a monogamous relationship and looking for political involvement. Straight Left groups i found alienating because of assumptions of correctness and knowledge; i wasn't then aware of any gay ones. I was (am) white middle-class with some knowledge of feminist theory and very little knowledge of socialist theory. I felt inarticulate and wanted to find a group with whom to work and learn in which my lack of knowledge and inexperience could be changed. I had recently started going to a gay consciousness-raising group which though challenging and supportive wasn't all that i wanted. It was at this moment that i read *Achilles Heel* No. 1. I was excited to read material by a group of men who acknowledged the importance of feminist and gay politics in their lives:

Hidden too is the history of men's more collective and public struggle around sexual politics. Central to any account must be the history of gay men, gay culture and gay struggle – both for personal freedom and for the transformation of society. Over the centuries gay men have faced the deeply contradictory position of being men in a male-dominated society and at the same time defying the assumption of 'natural' heterosexuality upon which so much patriarchial power is based. Again responses to this contradiction have varied, but since the late nineteenth century at least, a gay consciousness has persistently challenged notions of masculinity which are relevant to all men. In this collective our own histories have been heterosexual on the whole. So has the history of the men's movement. We feel it is important to acknowledge our debt to the gay movement over recent years and voice our hopes towards the development of relationships between the two movements. For the journal we see the raising and discussion of the whole issue of heterosexuality and gayness as crucial and hope gay men will regard it as open for participation and contribution.
      Achilles Heel No.1 'Editorial – Creating a Men's Politics'

I wrote a letter of support in which i said '*I have recently been moving towards a desire to widen my political awareness but the problem is how?*'followed by a comment on my, then held, feelings about being gay: '*i am gay, but i am also a man and would enjoy the company of men who were not gay. We are people first and our sexual orientation is secondary.*' A 'we are all humansexuals' position which i later revised. In a camp tag i criticised the proof-reading, or rather the lack of it. It was this that resulted in my being asked to take on the job of proof-reading some of the next issue. I agreed. In December 1978 i went, somewhat nervously, to my first editorial meeting. Initially my relationship was peripheral. I listened to some discussion and organised when and how material would be proof-read. I liked the men i met, they were warm, gentle, soft and articulate in expressing doubt and uncertainty. I was made to feel that i was contributing. At the beginning and end of meetings opportunities were created for more personal communication.

Through the gay consciousness-raising group i began to form relationships with gay men who were more politically aware than i. Much that i learned confirmed my own feelings, made me rethink and analyse many of the power and class assumptions of my upbringing, so that i was, perhaps, a little less naive by the time i met the collective than when i had first written to them.

After the second issue came out in spring 1979 i was asked if i would like to join the collective. I said yes. By now i wanted to see if it was possible to work with non-gay men this way. I liked the six men i'd met, even felt sexual desire towards some of them – an ongoing problem that, and not only for me – and decided that it was worth taking a risk. I'm sure that my being gay was part of their wanting me to join; political credibility can be a motivating force, but it was not the only reason, i also had a perspective that they did not. I felt sure that i was gay from an early age and grew up hiding parts of myself, experiencing a process of subterfuge in a particularly focused way. Such an experience can have many debilitating effects but it does enable you to feel the distortions of the world. Later when i read or heard sexual/political theory i recognised within it elements from my own life. For the other men on the collective it was different. Whilst they had strong emotional and sometimes sexual relationships with men they saw their relationships with feminist women as primary. Often their experience and understanding of sexual politics was developed through their interaction with socialist/feminist women or through their friends in the gay movement.

For the next four years we struggled together, argued, shared love, gained strength and saw the rise of Thatcherism. The journal, from the response it received, fed into a widespread need. The support given in terms of letters and contributions from these islands and from abroad was very rich. This, combined with our commitment, enabled us to continue despite the increasing harshness of the political and economic climate. The collective grew until we were twelve with varying relationships to contributors and interested individuals. The journal was very much a part of all our lives. Which is not to say that there weren't difficulties. We did challenge and criticise each other. At times i despaired, at others i was deeply happy. My relationship with these men became part of the fabric of my life as we followed each other's changes over the years.

The Collective

In some ways we were a unified group. We were all in men's groups; we held a basic commitment to exploring the challenges of feminism and gay politics; we were creating and working out a real anti-sexist way of living; we held a commitment to the ideals of socialism; we were exploring and creating supportive relationships with men; and interested in blowing the gaff on masculinity. In other ways we were a diverse group who experienced the pains and frustrations of collective working. Differences would appear sharply. Many were the contradictions but rich was the hope that we could find ways of exploring or resolving them. Ways that would enable, support and encourage other men to find, or begin to find, patterns of living that were not oppressive to women and other men. High-flown ideals. Overweening ambition, maybe, but we attempted it and did create openings that had not been seen by many men before.

Towards the summer of 1979 Ian joined the collective; now we were eight. Both Pauls were involved with childcare, Andy and Steve were single-parent fathers. James and Vic lived in mixed houses, Ian lived in a squat and i shared a hard-to-let flat with another gay man. All of us were involved in radical politics, some of us were into therapy, all went to the cinema, ate, slept, made love, had sex, and attempted to work out our politics.

Initially i went through a period of discovery whilst we prepared and discussed issue 3. This was going to focus on children. I was not involved in discussions leading to this decision as they had taken place prior to my joining, but i accepted it once i understood where it came from:

The collective article in Achilles Heel number 1 'creating a men's politics' was an attempt to begin the task of saying were we'd got to. And by the time Achilles Heel number 2 was finished it felt like we'd completed getting out the essential backlog of ideas we'd half-privately been accumulating all this time. So, for issue number 3 we've let others have more of a chance and have published material that doesn't entirely reflect our views.
                    Achilles Heel No.3 'Notes From the Collective'

For this issue i was primarily involved in editorial discussion and production. We would meet fortnightly, increasing to weekly once production deadlines evolved. Much of the discussion was around the collective's relationship with and towards the feminist and gay movements; this discussion was rather diffusely reflected in the published issue but a lot of taking stock took place during this period. To some extent i was seen as an 'expert' on the gay movement, its current feelings and developments. I was uneasy about this and tried to discourage it by relating my personal experiences rather than generalising. Also i was seen as someone with access to experience they didn't have and within situations where i felt supported i did initiate or was involved in discussions on homophobia and gayness. Often it was hard, especially when i questioned their own heterosexuality. Some of these men had an intellectual commitment to gayness whilst others were interested in exploring the gayness within themselves.

A strongly felt difference was that i had lived experience of, an innate understanding of, the oppression of patriarchy. Whilst for them it is a reality more deeply buried, one that, initially at least, is experienced less consciously. They were much more concerned with learning to lose power, to break through a deadening masculinity. This, perhaps, polarises it too sharply, for i too am a man. I also had to learn, understand and combat the wiles of patriarchy, particularly in situations with women. I remember that i had to organise publicity for two performance artists, a woman and a man, and quite unthinkingly i gave greater credit to the man. Or in meetings i would not listen to women, interrupt them or dismiss their contributions. I had to learn to see my own sexism. Also i had very real difficulties with the forms of masculinity imposed on me as a gay man. This usually expressed itself in self-doubt or confusions about role play – was i, yet again, falling into age-old patterns? But i did feel nearer to the other side of the coin and their obtuseness was, at times, difficult to bear.

These men had a different relationship to feminism from me. My position was one of being politically united with feminism, experiencing some of the oppressions suffered by women whilst having some of the power of being a man. For them, their desire to change developed from a realisation within and from their relationships with feminist women. There appeared to be a lot we could learn from and give to each other; sharing the experiences of our lives was important in this and in developing our abilities to feel the political connexions between our personal lives and a wider social sphere. To assert the primacy of sexual politics in the struggle for socialism.

Working Together

Meetings tended to be warm and affectionate even though they were often heated. We would arrive around 7.30pm, welcome each other, often with an embrace and talk about ourselves until everyone was there. We would usually begin by reading and talking about letters received or matters relating to the last issue, then we would draw up an agenda of things to discuss. This discussion would usually be about articles in progress or received, the issues they raised, the editorial or the theme. We tended to focus on issues and how they related to us personally – going in before coming out – whilst attempting to ensure some level of theoretical debate. Meeetings again ended with embraces. Occasionally we would all go off to the pub. Issues and contradictions were always coming up, if not in meetings then elsewhere:

> *After an Achilles Heel meeting we decided to go for a drink in a local pub. I was wearing a badge with the word gay clearly readable on it. Immediately i was picking up hostile reactions – men staring at me, nudging their friends, talking about me knowing i could hear them. I became very tense, standing taut, staring them out if i caught a man's eye. I felt very uncomfortable and intimidated. I stayed close to the men i was with wondering what they'd do if something happened. Chris held my hand seeing my tension and asked if i wanted to leave. I said i was feeling threatened by the reactions of the men around us but that it was our space as much as theirs. We continued talking, finished our drinks and left. Outside on the pavement we all said goodbye, hugging and kissing as usual, at the same time other people from the pub were also leaving, moving past or around us. I was glad that i was travelling home with Chris, two felt safer than one alone.*
>
> *In this situation i expected these men, my brothers, to be aware of the hostility that was being presented and to be supportive to me. It is important that non-gay men sense the hostility that we receive and support us in dealing with it.*
>
> Achilles Heel No.5 'Live Dangerously: Homophobia and Gay
> Power'

When i wrote that article we had much discussion about how non-gay men can learn to empathise with gay men's oppression. Within the collective it was felt vital that men in the men's movement be able to do this as part of developing an awareness of how oppressive men are to each other.

By the time the fourth issue appeared in 1980 we had defined how we saw the collective:

> *Achilles Heel (formerly men's free press) is a writing, and publishing support group committed to supporting men in writing about men's politics and socialism. Publication of this journal is the major focus for our coming together and we do aim to encourage contributions from outside the collective.*
>
> *While hesistant to label (and so limit) our influences and ambitions for Achilles Heel, our individual and collective histories are heavily influenced by socialist and anti-sexist experience and theory.*
>
> Achilles Heel No.4 'About Achilles Heel'

This had grown out of work during the previous year when we made the decision to concentrate each issue around a central theme. The collective continued to grow; now we were twelve. Other men coming in much the same way i had. This affected power relationships and tended to equalise them. When i first joined i was a newcomer amongst a group of men with a shared sense of history, by the fourth issue i was one of the older members and my sense of newness had long since gone. Although we did not consciously attempt to set up power blocs, trying to remain open to change, we would coalesce around particular issues. Those of us who felt strongly would unite. This happened most obviously around articles.

There was usually at least one contentious article submitted for each issue. If several of us didn't like the article we would become a group against those who wanted the article included and vice versa. We would attempt to work with the writer of the contentious article on the difficult areas until a majority of the collective felt able to agree to publication. Such differences were painful, particularly if the writer was a member of the collective.

Issue 4 was the first time another openly gay man was involved in the production of an issue. He was a man i knew through a gay affinity group who wrote an article for the issue about his experience of working in a factory. It was good for the collective to experience working with another gay man and it lifted the pressure from me. His being there gave me strength. During this time my own writing was encouraged and from being involved in editorial discussions or the preparation of editorial statements i initially produced some poems for inclusion and then articles for the issues on violence and sexuality. Writing was often hard as articles usually had to go through a number of drafts and might not be printed. We were tough on each other, feeling it was important that our work clearly expressed our meanings. There were times when we each had to cope with resentments about criticism. It was in this that our experiences of being in men's groups was invaluable, for the way we discussed contributions – be they our own or from outside the collective – was with an awareness of wanting to draw out and construct rather than critically demolish.

For issue 5, on male violence, we established a separate men's group within the collective so that we could work on ourselves in terms of the issues of male violence. These meetings alternated with production meetings so progress on the issue was slow. Over a period of six months we met fortnightly to share our experiences of violence or of being violent. Some of these meetings were taped and emerged in the issue in the editorial and in an article based on the transcripts. It was an important process, for how could we, as men, publish an issue on male violence without having explored on a personal/political level the issues ourselves?

This way of working was, for me, one of the most exciting things about beng involved with this group of non-gay men. There was a complete recognition of the complexities of our realities, combined with a desire to work through some of the complexities without reducing everything to a banal compromise.

Sex and Desire

Something very complex was the issue of sexual desire towards men within the collective. There is a theory of the constructed relationship of gay and non-gay men which always ties us to the subordinated/desiring role and them to the superior/admired one. I did not wish to uphold this theory, desiring, in practice, the creation of real personal/political identification. It was not a real problem until Ian joined the collective to work on issue 3. Up to that point i had experienced pleasure in being affectionate with these men, had occasional masturbation fantasies about them but felt that we were a band of brothers. With Ian it was different. I became infatuated with him. He was very confusing. I felt shy of him yet he obviously liked me, liked being with me, liked giving me a hug. But i felt unable to push it any further without any clear signals from him. I felt stupid spending so much time thinking about him; it was like being back at school. Would he be at the next meeting? Could i sit next to him? If the meeting was in the East End would he give me a lift home? If the meeting was at my place would he stay behind? Would we make love? etc, etc. He did stay behind after one meeting and we did talk about love – not mine for him – then, after a long silence, he left. I wrote poems about him but never gave them to him. I felt angry with myself. It was so completely fruitless. I knew that he was a love object but that didn't remove the desire.

In direct contrast when Chris joined the collective a year later there was an immediate affinity between us. He knew gay men, was close to a gay man in his men's group and was open to exploring his own feelings. We would see each other outside of meetings and developed a closeness which has changed but not been lost over the years. I desired him and he had feelings of desire for me. We were regarded for a while as lovers (or almost as lovers) by the rest of the collective. We were always together in meetings, often arriving or leaving together, we touched a lot and talked easily. There was sharing between us. We first slept together when we went to Bristol for the 1980 anti-sexist men's conference. In Chris's own words we 'melted'. The sleeping together was delightful, sex was more problematic. Chris didn't wish to experiment with me – for him sex and love were tied in a gordian knot – yet his sexual experience with men was so limited that it couldn't, at one level, be anything else. I was dangerous and safe. He wanted to experience pleasure, give me pleasure, express his feelings physically, but if he did did it mean he was gay? When i showed Chris the first draft of this essay he felt that i presented him as more confused than he was. He also wanted me to be more explicit. I have attempted to convey that we were lovers, that for a time we did melt into each other. It was after Bristol that it became clear, to both of us, that the sex didn't work. I didn't mind, at least we had both taken the risk. Unlike my experience with Ian our relationship was much more mutual, one in which we established boundaries together.

I was also aware, at times, of reciprocal feelings of desire amongst other members of the collective. When we were working well together an element of sexual desire was expressed in our physicality. Our differing experiences of sexuality were valuable. My sexual life was quite different from theirs but that didn't mean i couldn't discuss it, nor was i put down for it. But like everyone else i think my more *intense* emotional/sexual relationships occurred outside of the collective. What did happen was that we validated, in a non-verbal, tactile sense, our pleasure in each other's physical being. I do not know if there is such a thing as radical male bonding or if in some way all groupings of men are oppressive by their very nature, but i do know that it is possible within our lives to create relationships which are of such depth that we can continue to struggle and survive.

Reasons

Despite political differences, changing awareness, power shifts within the collective, we were a support group to each other. We had a structure within which we could challenge, ask without fear and explore the difficulties of living. This meant that we brought our experiences of external pressures into the collective discussion. Part of this external pressure on me as a gay man was criticism for working with non-gay men – though they were not called that by my critics. The question would be: Why was i putting my energies into Achilles Heel when our own struggles needed support? I would respond to this in two ways. One was defensive in that i pointed out that Achilles Heel was not my only political activity and i would go on to describe the other work i did with lesbians and gay men. If i felt stronger i would argue about the importance of establishing relationships with non-gay men who supported the gay movement. Over the years my feelings about working with non-gay men have changed. Initially my involvement was unthought out, since then i have come to recognise more deeply the political importance of gay and non-gay men working together.

I would rather work, in some areas of my life, with the men of Achilles Heel or men like them than with some of my gay brothers with whom i have no connexion other than a liking for sex with men. It goes back to the personal is political. I have more in common in terms of how i live, how i want to live, how i work, how i want the future to be with some anti-sexist men than i do with gay men whose lifestyle is based on consumerism – even if it is consuming the pink economy.

This is not to refute the validity of gay socialist-based autonomous work, for without such work it is not even possible to conceive of gay and non-gay men working together. We live a contradiction in that being self-identified around our sexuality we discover that although labelling can give us strength it can also constrict. This means that in order to work out our politics it is not enough to say 'I am gay'. I'm a socialist and my dreams of how i would like the world to be are shaped by this. It is a dream i feel i share with some, though not all, gay men. To say that you are gay is not always to say that you are radical, it is an acknowledgement that you are an outsider within society as we know it but no more.

'Ah, yes,' said a friend recently, 'but when the barricades, or whatever, go up the non-gay men can slip away to their grey suits safe in their conformity but gay men will never be safe. Even if they try to blend in they'll be found out and sent to the camps along with the rest of us.' I refuted this. I don't think politically committed non-gay men do have a choice. They know it is in their own interest, as some gay men also recognise it is in their own interest, to struggle together for what we believe.

*

From 1979 to the end of 1982 i was deeply involved in the collective. By the time issue 6/7 on sexuality was in the bookshops i knew the time had come for a rest. I was tired, it was time for others to take over, to carry on. We were involved in discussions about change, the increasingly harsh political and economic climate meant that to survive we had to reach a wider audience, increase our distribution. This would mean changes in the format of the journal as well as new members joining the collective. I was uncertain as to how much of all this i could deal with. The need to withdraw became very strong and over several months i left the collective. I was not alone in this. It was as though part of a cycle had been completed. It had reached an end and as with most endings there was sadness. I still see and am close to some of the men i worked with throughout those years. The work i do now would not be what it is without my experience of having worked in Achilles Heel with those particular men. I have no regrets.

Achilles Heel is currently looking for contributors. Copies can be obtained from: Achilles Heel, 79 Pembroke Road, London E17 9BB.

An extract from:

The Conversations of Cow

Suniti Namjoshi

Introduction

The Conversations of Cow is a lyrical satire describing the adventures of the first person narrator, Suniti, with Cow. Cow has a disconcerting habit of undergoing transformations. She has been in turn a lesbian cow, a lesbian cow disguised as a white man, called Baddy, a self-possessed woman, called B or Bhadravati, who in a gentler phase verges on a wood nymph or a minor goddess. In this form, she has just engaged in a lyrical love affair with Suniti.

At this point, Suniti asks about the logical development of their relationship: should they, for example, get married? B seizes on the idea gleefully and threatens to become a man from Mars. (Mars because Suniti has just expounded her private theory that all men come from Mars. A theory that is able to explain men's attitudes to the other planetary creatures: pigs and poodles, bats and babies, women and children.) B decides to become Bud; and Suniti, as usual, is greatly distressed....

The Conversations of Cow

At breakfast B has turned into what is unquestionably a Martian. I don't like it. I scowl at first, then turn my back. B seems impervious. But when Madeleine comes in, B jumps up, hovers about her, and tries to see that she has everything she wants. The fact that B is making her comfortable in her own house doesn't escape my notice, but Madeleine refrains from pointing it out. She waits for someone to explain matters.

B suddenly sticks out a hand. 'I'm Bud, you know. Glad to meet you. – And this is Suniti.' He pushes me forward.

'I believe we've met,' I say feebly. Madeleine blinks, smiles and disappears.

Bud and I are left facing one another. 'Well,' he says, 'I'll just bring down the suitcases. Then we're ready to go.'

I don't say anything, but then he hasn't waited for an answer.

While I'm waiting, Margaret and Charlotte walk into the room. I leap to my feet.

'Margaret,' I expostulate, 'you've got to stop this.'

'Stop what?'

'Bud. He has taken over.'

From the expression on their faces I can see that they understand exactly what has happened, but they don't seem worried.

'What has he been doing?'

'He's been drinking coffee and is fetching the suitcases.'

'Well, that's quite helpful of him, isn't it?' Charlotte offers.

'But it's the way he's been doing it.'

Just then Bud comes down. He kisses Margaret and Charlotte rapidly, says 'Thanks for everything,' grabs me by the elbow and rushes me out, shouting, 'Come on, Suniti, let's go.'

He has the car keys and has started the engine before I can stop him.

'Just a minute,' I say. I don't want to be rude, but this is really too much. I go back to the house.

'Margaret, Charlotte, Bud has turned into a Man from Mars. What shall I do?'

'Well, you don't have to go with him,' Charlotte says.

'But he has my car keys. He's revving up the engine. What shall I do?'

'Ask him for the car keys,' Charlotte suggests.

'But that means a confrontation....Oh Margaret.'

Margaret comforts me. 'It's all right, Suniti. He's still B. Why not play along and see what happens?'

'All right,' I answer, but I have my misgivings. I kiss them good-bye, and look about for Madeleine, but she's nowhere in sight. I feel sadder than ever.

I go up to Bud and demand the car keys.

'Sure,' he replies, 'but you don't have to be so uptight about it, you know.'

I put the car into gear and drive off. Bud beside me wears a stolid face, he looks immovable.

After an hour or so, when we've had some coffee and I've paid for my own, I feel better, though what I object to is that his letting me pay seems a kindly concession. I remind myself that B is lurking in him somewhere, but it's difficult. He seems hopelessly alien.

When we get to Montreal and stop at a hotel, I try to check in while Bud stands quietly looking over my shoulder. But the clerk at the counter addresses him exclusively. I put it down to his allying himself with a fellow Martian. But what am I to make of the waitress at dinner who behaves as though only Bud existed and I was the furniture?

At last it's over. We can go to our room. I shall talk to Bud. Surely in the end B will emerge?

'B,' I say severely, 'this has gone on long enough.'

But Bud merely puts his arms around me and gives me a kiss. I draw back. 'Stop it!' I exclaim.

'Why?' he asks.

'Because it's not what I want.'

'But is that important? You don't have to do anything. Just lie back....' As I'm about to lose my temper, his face breaks into a mischievous grin, the expression softens.

'B,' I exclaim gladly, 'B, you're back.' But when I put my arms about her, there's an incongruity – B's head and Bud's body. I sit on the bed and stare at her.

'What have you done?'

'Nothing,' B says. 'What's the matter, Suniti? You look so perplexed, and all day long you've been so very bad-tempered.'

'But your body....' I begin.

'Don't you like me as I am?'

'Well, yes, no.'

B is smiling. 'Do you know, the trouble with you is that you're very conventional.'

I pull myself together. 'That's not fair, B. It's not just me. When I'm with Bud in public, I become an appendage, a secondary person.'

'Oh come on, Suniti, why not look at it differently? You share in his status. When we return to Toronto with Bud at your side, you'll be a different person.'

I hadn't thought of that.

'B,' I wail. 'How on earth am I to explain to Bud?'

'There's nothing to explain. You've caught yourself a live Martian. It's perfectly normal.'

'B,' I'm pleading with her now. 'Please dispense with Bud. When Bud is around, I feel uncomfortable.'

'But Suniti,' she says, 'that's your problem, not Bud's.'

'But he does it on purpose.'

'What?'

'Taking advantage of his superior status.'

B draws herself up. 'Bud, I'll have you know, is a nice person. And you, my friend, are an out and out snob and very status conscious.'

I feel defeated. Perhaps B is right. I feel awful. Privately I think there isn't much to choose between B and Bud.

Suddenly B turns gentle. She puts an arm around me. 'Would you like to be Bud?'

'No, I've already told you, I wouldn't.'

'There, you see, it's hard being Bud. It's generous of me to agree to be Bud.'

This is so outrageous that for a moment I can't think of an answer, but I manage to ask 'Very well then, what are the duties and obligations of Bud?'

'Oh, the usual ones, being strong, successful, right and noble.'

'And the duties and obligations of Bud's partner?'

'Oh you mean Sue's? The complementary ones – being weak, incompetent, uncertain and inferior.'

'B, you know that's nonsense. An incompetent Sue would be useless to Bud. And in any event, I don't want to be a Sue or a Bud!'

'Yes dear.'

'Who was that?'

'Whoever you like, dear.'

'No, tell me, who are you at this moment?'

'But if you can't tell the difference, how does it matter?'

I don't know what to say, but I have to say something. I adopt a weary and patient tone. 'Of course it matters. Bud is a Martian, B isn't.' But even I can't keep a straight face over this piece of evasion. Bud is giggling, and I join her.

I don't sleep very well. What difference does it make whether B is B or B is Bud? But it does. It makes a difference to me. B is just B, but when Bud does something, he's backed by the forces of the Martian Empire.

'B,' I mutter, prodding him in the back. 'You're backed by the forces of the Martian Empire.'

B grunts.

That night I dream that the Jovians have invaded. They're unthinkably gigantic and unbelievably monstrous. Buddy and I are comrades in arms and giving battle. As we cower in a cave together I feel a sudden upsurge of fellow feeling.

'Buddy,' I exclaim, throwing an arm around his shoulders, 'compared to the Jovians you don't seem at all alien.'

Buddy responds by punching me lightly. 'You're a good chap, Suniti. Sometimes I forget you're not a Martian. When the war is over, why don't you take out proper papers? Become one of us? We'd have a good time together – two gay Martians exploring the world.'

I'm annoyed. I want to say, 'I guess I was wrong. Perhaps there isn't much difference between Martians and Jovians.' But it's the wrong time to say it. The Jovians are upon us.

*

I had half hoped that B might have tired of being Bud. She hasn't. I glare at her. But Bud is being pleasant.

'Good morning,' he says nicely. 'How are you feeling this morning?'

'Terrible thanks.'

'Why?'

'I would like Bud to go away and B to return. Oh it's not that I dislike Bud,' I add hastily, 'but he tends to bully me. B is much nicer.'

'But that's not true, Suniti. B reduced you to a small poodle, whereas all I do is make you irritable.' He looks vulnerable and hurt. I wonder if he's about to start crying. I put an arm around his shoulder.

'Well, since you're B anyway, I'll treat you exactly as though you were B. Then I'm sure we'll get on together.'

'All right, but only in private.'

'What?'

'Well in public I have to uphold the ancient traditions of the Martian Empire.'

'Oh to hell with you!' I'm angry. At this point I don't care whether I lose B or Buddy or both.

Buddy capitulates. 'Oh all right, I won't uphold the ancient traditions, but don't blame me if we get into trouble.'

'What do you mean?'

'Well, the Martians don't like it if any of their number goes native. There are severe repercussions....'

I see his point but I'll be damned if I concede it. 'Well, it's your own fault then for being a Martian.'

Buddy looks glum. 'Yes, Suniti, it's a terrible burden.'

We breakfast in silence.

'What shall we do?' he asks at last.

'Well we can't go to a lesbian bar, not this time. You wouldn't be welcome.'

'No,' he says. 'It's not fair. Haven't you any friends who would make me welcome?' He has that little boy look again.

'Several,' I mutter, but I'm thinking in particular of Amy Rose-Blossom. She would dote on him. I telephone her.

'Come on,' I tell him. 'We'll look around the city, and later we'll pay a visit. We've been invited to lunch.'

We walk about the city. He makes a point of being conspicuously ungallant. I pretend not to notice, but I find it tiresome.

Eventually he asks, 'Who are we visiting?'

'Someone who will like you.'

'Why?'

'She likes Martians.'

'What all Martians? Without discrimination?'

'Yes. She runs a home for them.'

'Oh you mean for the discarded and the disabled.'

'She thinks all Martians are in some way disabled. Something to do with the Jovian Wars. She thinks they need to be nursed and coddled.'

'Oh. You know, Suniti, I'm not at all sure I'll get on with your friend...' but they get on famously. Amy makes a fuss about him, and Bud relaxes and simpers and smirks.

I leave them together telling Bud I'll meet him at the hotel. I walk through the streets. It's the first time in days I've been by myself. I feel luxuriously anonymous.

*

But when I return to the hotel, I find that Bud is already back. He grins at me, 'Mrs Rose-Blossom's treatment does a world of good. You should try it, Suniti.'

'No,' I shake my head at him. 'The full treatment is for Martians alone. Amy says women don't need it. Amy says women are tough.'

But I feel relaxed and reasonably good tempered. We go out to eat and are nice to each other. As we're leaving the *maître d'hôtel* says, 'Bring her again. She's beautiful.'

Bud looks smug. 'There, Suniti. Aren't you pleased?'

'No. If you went into a parking lot with a foreign car, it's exactly what the attendant might say to you.'

Bud's face falls. 'You're very hard to please, you know.'

'So are you. You'd be pleased if I were pleased. What you want is happy acquiescence.'

'Well, why not? I could spend my life trying to please you, and you could spend yours being pleased. We'd live happily forever. Doesn't it sound good?'

'No, what you need is a stone companion, smiling happily for ever and ever.'

'No, what I need is a metal one, smiling happily when I push a button.' Bud smiles suddenly, 'After all, there are times when you've wanted one too, haven't you?'

'Wanted what?'

'A robot companion.'

I consider the matter. 'Well, be one then. After all, your function in life is to please, isn't it?'

'No, it isn't.'

'But only a moment ago you were saying....'

'That I'd like to please you? Yes, but only when it's convenient. And not as a robot. Why don't you be one?'

'What? A robot? You'd be bored, Buddy. What would you do for conversation?'

'For intellectual stimulus I'd seek out the society of my fellow Martians.'

'And what would I do?'

'You could join the local branch of the Robots' Club.'

By this time we're back at the hotel.

'Buddy,' I tell him quietly, 'I'm not a robot.'

'Suniti,' he answers, 'I'm not an alien.'

'Who are you then?'

'I think probably I'm really a woman. I would like to be one.'

I think of B, but there's no sign of her. Bud is being very much himself.

'Why?'

'It's less difficult.'

'Oh well, what's to stop you? Be a woman then.'

'Do you think I would make a good one?'

'No.'

'Why not?'

'You have the wrong habits.'

Bud seems depressed, but he quickly recovers.

'Are you a good woman?'

What can I say? 'No,' I tell him, 'I'm an unsatisfactory one.'

Suddenly B is grinning – it is B isn't it? – she puts an arm about me. 'Suniti,' she says, 'I'll tell you a secret, I also am an unsatisfactory Martian.'

'Oh, you do very well.' I pat her on the back.

But she feels I haven't been suitably impressed. 'I'll tell you another thing, and this is top secret, a well-guarded one – all Martians are unsatisfactory ones.'

I laugh. 'But B, that's a well-known fact.'

She looks put out. 'Well, at least you'll concede that you and the Martians have something in common.'

I smile, but it's an unsatisfactory solution. At last I ask, 'Are you trying to tell me that Men from Mars are really women?'

'Yes. You've got it at last.'

'But B, why do they behave so differently from women?'

'Lack of opportunity and education, my dear.'

B is grinning, I grin back; but late that night when B asks me, 'Suniti, what would you really like?' all I can say is, 'B, I need to be by myself for a bit; I would very much like to be left alone.'

EXIT 10: an allegory

Diana Chapman

Moving inexorably towards Earth is a spaceship. It is programmed for an orbit well above Earth to avoid the load of detritus that homo sapiens is already spewing into the atmosphere. Aboard is the Scientific Officer of a minor department of the Galactic Civil Service and It's attendant Robot. 'It' since It incorporates several sexes in It's own person. For the purposes of this narrative It shall be called God.

The sad truth is that God set up Planet Earth several aeons ago as part of a series of galactic experiments. It only had six days in which to do it and rather skimped the final stages. It is now returning to observe progress after an interval of time which by It's own time scale is but an evening gone, but by human time is a thousand ages.

The Robot knows its job and brings the spaceship to a docking point a suitable distance above Earth. It then activates the ship's giant scanner to search out an area of significant activity on the planet. Before long the image of a huge arena appears on the screen. God and the Robot look at it with interest. Into the arena from a door out of sight below the scanner stream a mass of men and women jostling and arguing. Ahead of them set in a great curving wall are doors marked 'Exit', and each Exit has a number. In front of each Exit is a Guardian who stands on a pile of old books. On each Guardian's head is a great crested helmet, their torsos are encased in moulded corselets and they sport huge ornamented codpieces. Their feet are encased in terracotta boots.

At each side of the arena are blackboards around which the humans jostle to read the instructions chalked on them. These tell the humans through which gate they should go to participate in various activities.

Through Exit 3 for example, people are turned into philosophers, psychiatrists and used-car salesmen. Exit 7 offers war and all its attendant professions. Exit 10 is labelled: 'Heterosexuality' (inc. breeding, domestic duties etc.). As the docile humans line up at the various Exits the guards check their suitability for admission by a cursory glance at their genitals. This rather rough and ready test is the basis upon which one in two of the applicants is turned away and waved towards Exit 10. The majority of those thus rejected shrug their shoulders and trudge off towards the only Exit apparently available to them.

'That's odd,' says God, intently watching the screen back in the spaceship. 'D'you notice, Robot, all the ones turned away and pushed towards Exit 10 are female. Why do you suppose that is?'

'If I may suggest, Omniscience,' murmurs the Robot, 'perhaps that is all the female is fit for. You did after all, create the male first and then remove one of his ribs to provide raw material for creating the female.'

'What if I did,' says God testily, 'I still endowed her with intelligence equal to his. If I'd only intended her as a breeding machine, domestic servant and sexual receptacle, I'd have designed her quite differently. Six arms and a built-in hydraulic lift for a start. Oh look – some of the females are arguing. Adjust the sound, Robot, this should be interesting.'

In front of the Exits some of the women are arguing with the great armoured Guards.

'Why can't I go through here?' demands one woman.

'Why aren't MEN sent through Exit 10?' shouts another.

The Guardian pushes up his visor and grins down at them. 'You don't want none of this nonsense that goes on through here,' he says. 'You're not meant for it. A strong man, a good screw and lots of babies, that's all you need, and when you go through there –' he jerks his thumb towards Exit 10, '– you'll get 'em.'

'What about MEN?' a woman persists. 'If sex and babies are so bloody marvellous, why don't you go through Exit 10 too?'

The Guard looks puzzled. 'They don't need to darlin', they get all that anyway. Y'see, after you lot goes through Exit 10, you go into the Automatic Brainwash. That makes you forget any daft ideas you might have had like jobs and independence and that, and the Moving Pathway takes you where the men are waiting and they pick you off.'

'Sounds horrible,' says a tall young woman.

''ORRIBLE!' shrieks the outraged Guard. 'It's yer DESTINY, and don't you fergeddid!'

'The hell with destiny,' another woman shouts, and makes a rush towards a forbidden door.

The Guard grabs her, roughly. 'Yer stupid cow,' he yells. 'Don't yer know what's good for yer? Look! Look at that!'

He jerks the woman round and her eyes follow the direction of his pointing finger. On the ground, some almost obliterated but some quite fresh, are ominous brown stains.

'That's blood that is. Blood of daft cunts like you who wouldn't go nice and easy through Exit 10. Don't argue wiv' me gel. I'm telling yer.'

As he lets go of her a light voice speaks from behind.

'Trouble Sarnt?' it enquires.

The Guard stands to attention. 'No,Sir. Just the usual few stridents, Sir. Don't want to go through the krek door,Sir.'

'My Dear Ladies' – the speaker is slender and handsome, his voice soft and his eyes kind. 'Be sensible. No reasonable person would go through any other gate but Exit 10 if they had a choice. If you only knew what lies beyond these others. The heat, the dust, the skirmishes, the smells, the PEOPLE – UGH! Whereas, on the other side of Exit 10 there is protection, love, rose gardens, gurgling pink babies, snowy nappies blowing in the zephyr –'

''Scuse me guv –' a woman breaks in, 'you make it sound everso nice. I take it you had no choice, but if you had would YOU go through Exit 10?'

The beautiful man flinches. 'CHRIST NO!' he shrieks and suddenly spotting a friend on the other side of the arena hastily makes his excuses and hurries away.

By this time the sun is low in the sky. Only a small group of defiant women remain in the arena. They are tired, hungry, thirsty and uncertain. Those Guards who remain are becoming irritable.

'Give 'em another five minutes,' mutters one, 'then we'll bloody well boot 'em through.'

The women overhear this and move uneasily away in the direction of Exit 10.

'I'm not going through there' says the tall one whose name is Amazonia. 'Didn't you hear what he said about the Automatic Brainwash?'

'Not much choice, is there luv?' an older woman replies. Her name is Domestica.

Suddenly one of the other women gives a shout, 'Hey, look over there!'

The women turn eagerly to where she is pointing and sure enough, beyond Exit 10 and half hidden under a bougainvillea tree, is a small opening.

'Come on women!' cries Amazonia, and the little band hurries towards the unlabelled Exit. They duck under the bougainvillea and find themselves in a cool, dark space. Ahead of them rises a short flight of stone steps at the top of which is a sturdy door lit by the flames of a fire burning in a cresset. They climb the steps and read by the firelight an inscription carved into the lintel of the door. It reads: 'All blokes abandon, ye who enter here'.

There are murmurs from the women: 'Right on!' 'Suits me!' 'Let's get through quick.'

'Yes,' cries Scholastica, a small, bespectacled woman. 'Hurry, the Guards are coming.'

Sure enough, pounding feet and shouts are nearing the door behind them. Amazonia gives the door a push and it swings open on well-oiled hinges. She holds it back and the women tumble through. Amazonia lets go of the door, it swings back and closes with a final clunk. On the other side the Guards beat and shout ineffectually. Amazonia and Scholastica smile at each other in relief.

'That was close,' Amazonia says.

'Yes,' replies Scholastica, 'but there's something odd. In the arena we are led to believe that there's only one Exit for us women, yet that's not true. Not only is there another Exit but the staircase is lit, the door hinges are oiled and the lock works. Strange isn't it?'

'It is,' replies Amazonia, 'and to be honest, I can't explain it. Some other time – let's catch up with the others and see what lies ahead.'

They join the rest of the women who are standing in a compound surrounded by a paling fence in which a gate swings in the night breeze. Beside the gate is another flaming cresset which illuminates a neatly printed notice bluetacked onto the gate post. The women crowd forward to read it. It says: 'CONGRATULATIONS. YOU HAVE NOW REACHED DEVIANT STATUS. THROUGH THE GATE LIES "BEYOND THE PALE". BON VOYAGE.' By the moonlight the women can see a path wandering away across a moor. Clouds scud across the moon and a chilly wind blows.

'Come on women,' says Amazonia. 'It looks a bit bleak but at least there's no Automatic Brainwash.'

Murmuring agreement, the women pass through.

Scholastica pauses to study the notice. 'Funny,' she mutters. 'The biro is unsmudged, the paper clean and –' she lifts a corner '– the bluetack fresh.' She shakes her head in a puzzled manner and hurries to catch up with the others having first carefully latched the gate.

The pilgrim band trudges steadily along the stony little path which dips and bends across the moor. They notice a gleam of light from a cottage, hear a dog barking and suddenly a fox darts across their path, an illict chicken in its mouth.

'Lucky sod!' grunts Domestica, 'me tripes are stickin' to me bleedin' backbone.'

Amazonia, who is in the lead, suddenly pauses. To their left a small path runs off ending in a small flat space. In the middle of the little space sits a Well.

'If you're all as thirsty as I am,' she says, 'that looks hopeful.'

'It could be poisoned,' someone says doubtfully.

Scholastica has walked over to the Well. 'I don't think so,' she says. 'See, here's a pile of plastic cups, a disposal bin and some wooden benches.' She sniffs the bucket and lowers it into the Well. There is a splash and Scholastica winds up the brimming bucket. 'Here goes,' she says, and tastes the water. 'It's fine,' she announces and finishes the cupful.

The parched women eagerly dip their cups in and drink. In the meantime Scholastica has spotted another little notice tacked to the Well side. 'Please do not leave litter and put all cups into the receptacle provided. Thank you.' The note is unsigned. Amazonia has strolled over and together they inspect it.

'Pity no one has left any litter,' observes Amazonia. 'If they had we might have some clue as to who has been this way before us. Tell me,' she turns to Scholastica, 'why did you hold out against going out of the arena by Exit 10?'

'I think there were two reasons,' Scholastica replies. 'First I had set my heart on being a molecular biologist. To be honest I was rather inspired by Rosalind Franklin, who was, you may remember, very shabbily treated by Crick and his colleagues over the discovery of DNA, and I became very resentful when those damn' great Guards kept pushing me away from the Science Exit. Then it occurred to me that there must be something fishy about the way the Guards reckoned the only way they could get us to go through Exit 10 was by blocking off every other. After all, if what lay beyond no. 10 was so bloody marvellous, we'd all be fighting to go through, not have to be herded. What about you?'

'Pretty much the same. I wanted to go through the Exit marked "WAR". I think now I was mistaken, but at the time it sounded exciting and dangerous, and a lot of kudos is given to those who do well in it, but the Guard pushed me back and said that women weren't meant to be brave or earn glory, that was only for men. Women were to shut up, do as they were told and have babies. ME have babies! I LOATHE babies! So I thought, "Hell, what AM I going to do?' then someone noticed that little Exit and I ran towards it like the rest of us."

Scholastica nods towards Domestica. 'Let's ask her why she came along.'

Domestica scratches her nose reflectively. 'Hard to say,' she says. 'All me mates was going towards Exit 10. They weren't game to argue with them great Guards, and there'd be no point anyway. We weren't brainy, we didn't want to do any of them posh things, we just wanted to do what was right and proper. So I went along wiv' me mates – but when I got near to that Exit 10, – cor, what a pong!'

'You could smell something?' queries Scholastica.

'Not 'alf. Terrible. Put me in mind of my poor Mother. Dirty socks, sweaty jockstraps, semen, blood, boiling nappies – the LOT. UGH!. It fair turned me up. "Dommie, me gel," I said to meself, "Don't get trapped like your poor Mum was, there must be another way out". Then I looked round and saw you lot heading towards that little Exit and I hared over and caught you up, and here I am.'

'It's a bit cold and cheerless out here,' says Amazonia. 'Are you sure you don't regret joining us?'

'Nah!' says Dommie scornfully. 'When did a bitta of fresh air ever hurt anyone? Or exercise come to that? Come on, we bin here long enough. Let's get going.'

The Deviant women, for such they had now become since they passed Beyond The Pale, plod on. The path skirts settlements from which dogs bark angrily and men in nightcaps jeer from windows. The faint howl of wolves is borne on the night wind, but the air is sweet and the women don't lack courage. The path takes a dip into a forest. The little band, plunging into the trees, see firelight ahead and smell delicious smells of meat roasting and vegetables brewing. They come out of the trees into a clearing in the middle of which a great fire blazes enticingly, and on which meat fizzes and blackened cauldrons bubble. Set back amongst the trees are tents and shacks. Around the fire children frolic, dogs and cats squabble amicably and women are gathered, some tending the food, or repairing clothes. One sharpens arrows, another tunes a lyre, another skins a dead rabbit. The Deviant women pause, unwilling to disturb the household calm. One of the Campfire women looks up and sees them.

'Hello,' she calls. 'I say, you look fearfully done up. Come over by the fire and have some plonk – there's plenty of grub too. Come on.'

Thankfully the weary Deviants sink by the fire and accept beakers of wine. By this time their presence has attracted other Campfire women who gather round with eager questions.

'Where are you from? Where are your Men? What are your names?'

The exhausted Deviants look at each other and shake their heads.

'That's enough, girls,' the Campfire leader orders. 'The poor dears are exhausted and starving. Food and drink first and questions afterwards.'

The ravenous Deviants tuck in to bowls of delicious meat and vegetables and jacket potatoes and freshly baked bread, washed down with beakers of wine. At last, replete, they sit back. Several, regrettably, fall on their backs and doze off.

'Now,' the Campfire spokeswoman looks at them inquiringly, 'you must have come from the Arena?'

'Yes, we have,' replies Amazonia.

'So,' the Campfire leader glances round, 'where are your Husbands? You shouldn't be out in the cold and dark without Men to protect you.'

'None of us,' replies Amazonia, 'have Husbands.'

Consternation breaks out among the Campfire women. 'Impossible...couldn't have got this far...no women allowed out without one...!'

'Shut up, dears,' the Campfire leader asserts her authority. 'You MUST have Husbands – or at least some kind of Man. If, as you say, you came from the Arena, and I know of no other starting point, you would have to have come out via Exit 10 and the Automatic Brainwash in which case you couldn't have avoided collecting Husbands.' She pauses expectantly.

'Ah, but you see,' Scholastica breaks in, 'we DIDN'T go through Exit 10. We found another way.'

At this further dismay is voiced by the Campfire women. 'Can't be true...no other Exit for women...wouldn't want to even if there was...'

Scholastica interrupts them. 'We went through a little Exit half hidden by a bougainvillea, up a flight of steps and through a door which locked behind us.'

At this the Campfire women utter cries of disbelief. 'No such Exit...never heard of it...never saw it...not true...'

Suddenly a cool voice cuts across the other voices. 'Oh yes there is such an Exit. I noticed it, in fact I was tempted to take it but didn't have the courage. It's there alright, believe me.'

At this the Campfire women are dismayed. 'How awful for them...took the wrong turning...have to go back and start again...'

'Tell us,' someone calls, 'what happened after you went through the door at the top of the stairs?'

Amazonia and Scholastica look at each other, then Amazonia says, 'We found ourselves in a little compound surrounded by a paling fence in which there was a gate. A notice told us that we had by this time become Deviants and that once through the gate we were Beyond the Pale.'

'What utter nonsense!' cries the Campfire leader, 'you're not Deviants! How can you say such a thing? You're nice, normal, healthy women, like us.'

There is a slightly uneasy silence and Scholastica clears her throat. 'I would be interested to know,' she says, 'how you can tell Deviants from other women?'

The Campfire women mutter and shrug their shoulders. No one, it seems, knows the answer, but the cool voice breaks in from the shadows. 'I can tell you,' the speaker says. 'They are all six feet tall and dress exclusively in dungarees and nailed boots. They smell strongly of garlic and unwashed armpits.'

'Good Heavens, Sophistica!' someone says, 'how DO you know all this? Have you actually seen one?'

'My beloved Husband told me,' replies the hidden Sophistica languidly. 'He also says that they continually indulge in monstrous sexual practices which he'd be prepared to pay to watch; and if HE's prepared to shell out to watch something it must be worth watching.'

'I think Sophistica's having us on,' someone says doubtfully.

Amazonia has been casting round her mind for a diversion from this thorny topic. She leans forward. 'You say you go through the Automatic Brainwash and then collect a Husband. Why is that?'

'WHY? It's a prize, dear. Surely –'

'PRIZE! Bloody PENALTY more like!'

The interruption comes from a thin, worn-looking woman who has moved into the firelight. It was she who was dealing with the dead rabbit and there is blood on her apron and on the cleaver which she still holds.

'Oh Misandria,' someone says, 'you're so prejudiced. We all know that Fred's difficult, but he's your Husband, you must make allowances.'

'Allowances,' growls Misandria, 'I've made allowances for thirty fuckin' years and much good it's ever done me.'

'May we ask, Misandria,' it is Scholastica speaking, 'why you married him?'

'EH?'

Misandria is taken aback. No one has asked her to explain anything for years and words don't come easily.

'Hard to say after all this time. He was one of the Gatekeepers, I do remember that, all done up in his helmet and the rest of it. I was young then, I didn't notice the terracotta boots. Anyway, all the girls I knew were trooping through that Exit 10, so I just trailed along. No one told me there was any other way out.'

She pauses, searching her memory.

'You went through the Gate and then presumably through the Brainwash?' Scholastica prompts gently.

'Yer, thassit,' Misandria's face clears as memory comes back to her. 'There was this moving path and it took us into a tunnel with all soft lighting, rose coloured it was. As you went along there was all these pictures of them lovely men – Cary Groper, Charles Voyeur, Gregory Pecker – and it smelt nice...Channel Five I think it was. We all had earphones and there was lovely music and these soft voices, and they kept on and on saying things like, "Did the Earth move, Maria?"..."She had to lose them all to realise she loved Rhett...", and all the time there were diamonds and sapphires and rubies flashing into our eyes and when we got to the end the men were waiting to pick us off, and we were so softened up we couldn't even see 'em properly. And we couldn't see each other, us women, our mates, at all.'

'Then what happened?'

'I saw him, Fred, in his armour. High as a steeple, strong as Hercules. He grabs me arm and next thing I know I've signed a bit of paper and him and me goes to his house.'

She pauses and laughs. It is not a pretty sound.

'Jesus wept! He takes off his helmet and his corselet and his codpiece and what's left? I'll tell yer what's left. A plucked fowl with a couple of pickled walnuts and a chipolata between its legs. "Make me some soup," it whines, "I'm getting a cold".'

The Campfire women break into soothing noises. 'There, there, that's Marriage, dear. They're only Men after all.'

Misandria breaks away from their comfort with a great cry, 'That's it! They ARE only men; but they make out they're higher and stronger and greater then they really are, and they put their feet on our necks and make us eat shit, and we're expected to treat them like they was fuckin' God, and they're only men.'

She bursts into tears. The women crowd to comfort her but as they do a great yell of rage rents the air. Into the firelight rushes a small man. Balding with a hairy paunch, he clutches a towel round his middle. He spots Misandria in tears. 'Y' stupid cunt!' he yells, 'why haven't y' stoked the Aga? Where's me clean shirt? Why haven't y' pressed me trews? I TOLD y' ten bloody times I was going to the club tonight and I'd wanta hot bath. D'you expect me to do it myself or summat?' He stands, quivering with righteous indignation in the suddenly silent circle of women.

Misandria walks towards him, the blood-stained cleaver still dangling from her hand.

'For two pins,' she hisses, 'I'd slit you from arsehole to breakfast-time. For thirty years I've lived with you, cooked for you, nursed you, cleaned and laundered for you. Dried your tears when you wept and gritted my teeth when you screwed me. Well, get this Freddie boy, it's over. I'm through, I'm quitting, from now on you're flying solo.'

'Oh come on, Mizzie,' the man begins to whine, 'we're pals, you and me. We've had a few words now and again, but I'm yer Husband. Anyway,' he adds spitefully, 'y've nowhere to go.'

'Oh yes I 'ave.' Misandria gestures towards the watchful Deviants. 'I'm goin' with them. They've got sense AND they're not cluttered with bloody men.'

Fred looks, and for the first time takes in the presence of the Deviants. He begins to laugh.

'Y'daft cow,' he splutters, 'd'you know what they are? Them's Deviants. Dykes, lezzies, freaks, weirdos, they couldn't get a man if they –'

'Oh shut up, you crapulous little prick.'

The cool voice is strolling from the shadows into the firelight. She is tall and very beautiful. Her earrings glint in the light and a long black cloak hangs from her shoulders. She swings, her cloak swirling, towards her audience.

'Mizzie is quite right,' she proclaims, 'we put up with far too much from these bastards. Look at me!' – she pauses, and the Deviants murmur appreciatively. 'I've had three Husbands, and so many lovers I've lost count. I've done so many handjobs I've got tennis elbow and so many blowjobs my bridgework's wearing out. I've paid their bills, cleaned up their flats, cooked their meals and then had their girlfriends weeping on my shoulder. I think, darlings, like Mizzie, I've had enough. And you -' she turns to the Deviants, 'can count me in. By the way, Mizzie, bring that machete along, it might come in useful.'

A cry of protest goes up from the Campfire women.

'Sophistica – you CAN'T! Think of poor Cecil. He's your Husband after all.'

Sophistica raises her elegant hand. 'Sweetie, he won't even notice, he's too busy shagging his new secretary. She dotes on him, poor cow, but I think he's getting bored already. I see the signs.'

Silence falls. The Deviants mutter amongst themselves.

'Won't you stay with us?' asks the Campfire leader. 'It's quite cosy, really, and after a time you get used to the Husbands, they're not all like Mizzie's and Sophistica's.'

The Deviants shake their heads.

'I think we must be moving on, it will soon be sunrise,' says Amazonia.

'Where will you go?' someone asks.

The Deviants shrug their shoulders.

Amazonia says, 'We shall hope to find a place where we can set up our camp and be safe from men. Maybe we'll have to go to an island. One thing we're sure of, others have been this way before us, we are not as small a band as we seem.'

The little band of Deviant women with their two new recruits make their way out of the camp and on to the path. The Campfire women wave goodbye. Some frown and shake their heads disapprovingly, some look decidedly wistful. In the East the sky lightens with the first hint of dawn.

Meanwhile, back at the spacecraft, God is looking very downcast.

'Well, Robot,' It observes, 'that project went wrong pretty quickly didn't it? From all the other data you've given me it seems that the male of the human species is not only treating the female appallingly, but is making Earth a living hell for all the other creatures I put on it to keep the humans company. If it weren't against Regulations, I'd abort the whole sorry thing. As it is, I have to leave them to work out their own salvation – or damnation, most probably. I see they've learnt to split the atom, so it can't be long now.'

'If I might make a suggestion, Supremacy?' murmurs the Robot, 'your Illustriousness will no doubt be contemplating further projects in other parts of the Universe, with hope of a better outcome than this one?'

'Indeed, yes, Robot. Had you something in mind?'

'A mere notion,' said the Robot, deprecatingly. 'Among the lesser species on Earth, the arachnids are adaptable and in their way successful. Using their construction as a basis, but introducing the higher faculties...'

'Go on, Robot. I can see that with eight legs, many eyes and web-spinning facility, they have possibilities. What particular advantage had you in mind?'

'Merely that the female is bigger and stronger than the male – and devours him after copulation.'

'Robot,' says God, 'I think you've got something there. Set course for home. I'm going back to the drawing board.'

A Little Prison Journal

Robert Glück

On June 20 1983 I was arrested at the anti-nuclear blockade of the Livermore Laboratory. Here is a journal I wrote in the Santa Rita County Jail.

Monday morning: At 4.30 the clock radio flooded my bedroom with a Hungarian rhapsody faster than my unconscious could bale itself out. I got up, a thief in the night. I wrote support-people's phone numbers on my torso with a ballpoint, hid some migraine tablets and a few dollars in the lining of my corduroy coat, put on layers of clothing for cold nights and hot days, and bunched up a few plastic bags in case we were kept on a bus all day with no toilets. Denny slept. I could hear my breath. We had agreed to be nameless so I said goodbye to my wallet and driver's license. I kissed Denny awake and assured him that I'd be back in a day or two.

I belong to a gay men's affinity group called Enola Gay. Enola Gay leaves San Francisco in two cars and arrives in Livermore at dawn: a chill inland sunrise, purple clouds backed by a white sky. A suggestion sends us away from the legal demonstration down Vasco, along with twenty others. We stand in the middle of an alarmingly empty road. Other protestors drift by.

What if we don't get arrested? Then cars appear and we sit down and spread out; after we halt the first few cars we get up, excited, sing and chant, although sometimes the silence quiets us: fields, pastures, scrub oak, a horse. Eventually sixty or seventy cars back up.

An hour later: Too tired and hot for singing. We mill around. The cars wait listlessly. The heat buzzes – an audio dislocation induced by lack of sleep. The enormous fact, about two miles away, of Lawrence Livermore National Laboratory, which we never actually saw, dwarfs our human scale. The Lab heads our weapons production chain; it should twist the oaks, yellow the grass, call down a biblical darkness. These ordinary American fields and pastures depress me.

Then from out of nowhere leaps the Dance for Life Affinity Group blaring 4/4 from a portable tape deck. They grin, delighted, dancing hard in pairs, eye to eye in a 1970s time warp of tight disco – then hips gyrate and dancers spring singly across the asphalt in grand jétés.

At once two police cars pull up. Support-people stand back. We scramble down. A cop stands above us and puts us under (literally spreading out his palms over us so that we are under) arrest. Fear and awe. They are sitting us in a line in a dirt parking lot as though being arrested were merely a change of location. They take Richard and me together. Richard goes limp but in one motion the cop puts him in a half nelson and jabs a pressure point under his chin hard enough to break skin. I shout 'Shame on you – he didn't hurt you' right in the cop's face. I don't touch him (nonviolence training). My reprimand reminds me of my mom. He's about twenty-five, I'm thirty-six, and he *whines*, 'Then tell him to co-o-perate'.

Monday night: 1028 arrested. The women and men are separated: we're in huge circus tents! We can see the women's tents. We're in the middle of a field. This is not so much a jail as an internment camp for 1028 willing to do civil disobedience. Wind blows through the tent. Its green and orange striped walls are always moving; the big top is beige and red – the canvas sinks and bellies out. Lights mounted at the top insist on height and length, like a huge train station that pulses. At night we are also lit from outside by two floodlights but this is merely a flat agricultural valley and the darkness is just as penetrating. Two generators hum. A coil of barbed wire and a chalk line stand for our prison walls! Four hundred and fifty men sleep in narrow cots in one tent, the other is for eating. It was hot during the day, now it's cold and windy: all the clothes that nearly killed me on the bus I now appreciate and wear to bed.

Tuesday night: The District Attorney asks Judge Lewis for two years probation and either $250 or 11 days. If we do civil disobedience during probation we are liable for six months in jail. Probation is their strategy to break the peace movement. The penal system wants to isolate us, process us singly so that each is a child in the wrong whose personal fate has a haphazard, fairytale quality. We combat that strategy with solidarity: we decide to remain nameless John Does and to refuse arraignment. In other words, they are stuck with our collective body. Civil disobedience is an elegant subject, and elegant activity. Like sex, you do it with your body.

This is very strange – a male society, 450 mostly straight John Does of conscience. During high school I realized I wasn't one of the boys and made my life accordingly. Now my fear comes back. Still, there are no fag jokes and they seem to care for one another. A contingent of men's movement men sleeps right across the aisle. They are students, they stroke each other soulfully. It's back to high school for me, as though twenty years didn't happen, as though no one would talk to me, as though life happened elsewhere. I want to be in their ideal society. I trick myself into thinking that I'm unhappy and they're happy because they resemble the boys I once desired.

It's outrageously cold here; the blankets are a joke. Someone just put on a plastic bag, then his T-shirt. I bet that works. I think of Denny and warmth.

Wednesday morning: The sheriff comes to arraign us – we refuse – he could use force. When he doesn't we celebrate with a big circle, songs, chants. It becomes a ritual celebration twice a day. 'Listen up, gentlemen' – but few go.

In line for breakfast – so tired afterward I sink abruptly to the dirt. Rotten food: two tablespoons of *gruel* straight out of *Oliver Twist*, and vile coffee with beige cream that smells like rubber. The food is catered by the National Guard! Enola Gay discusses Linzertorte while eating lunch – the peanut butter spread so thin it doesn't discolour the bread. No one complains publicly (middle-class guilt even infects people who aren't).

Hot sun today. Naked men sunbathe on an old concrete loading ramp (distracting). I'm reading a Harlequin romance. Breezes undulate the red stripes. Some men jog, do yoga. Summer camp.

I got through to Denny on the phone – our conversation was broken, like a hospital visit: How *are* you? Fine. How are *you*? Fine, fine.

Wednesday night: Strategy meetings all day, not to mention the full moon ritual for those who want it, and workshops on topics like the Peace Movement in Europe – constant meetings, constant singing, a jail culture. We call ourselves the Santa Rita Peace Conference. But with gypsy tent colours, the crowded isolation and the mostly white population, this could be a displaced persons camp in Central Europe.

I no longer want to be a men's movement man. I just want to ravish and objectify their bodies, languorously naked and open in the heat. I select one and obsess. Beautiful men (some filled out with muscle, others whittled down to muscle) are mysterious to me. Sex is like that; when I'm attracted I assume the person *has* my attraction – a magical transfer of quality.

Every night a talent show: We shout, '*You too*, can be *sucked up*, in a *Tornado of Talent*,' as the next act wheels onto a stage marked out by ten cots stood on end. One act was a performance piece on *Star Wars*; Daniel Ellsberg did a magic trick, then reminded us to tell the press that we are protesting against the weapons to be deployed this fall. The MX, Cruise Missile and Pershing are first-strike weapons; they raise the stakes by giving a tremendous advantage to the side that attacks first. I imagine the motives of many people are more diffuse.

Lights out: Officially we are John Doe – a murmur of '*Night, John. Night, John*' – then jokes in the darkness: Why does a dog lick its cock? Because it can.

Thursday morning: I glance up: someone's shadow walks across the roof – red and beige. Joggers' shadows circle the striped tent walls. The entrance is a bright rectangle of blue. I'm surprised to be here still.

A trickle of men left, we applauded them, then chanted *No Fines, No Probation*. Still, I heard some guards chatting about electric cattle prods not leaving marks – ugh!

Friday: Enola Gay is fasting today, it's a relief. Noise and commotion: 400 men in a tent, bad food, cold nights; the judge won't budge. 'Listen up' – clapping and singing – I almost faint in the sun. An older man stumbled backward, fell. I saw his head bounce, heard it. I'm often tearful.

I begin a shipboard romance with a man named Paul. He's my age; my previous sex objects now seem like so many Hueys, Deweys and Louies. I'm back in my life. I start making friends. In one week I recapitulate my entire maturation.

They set up portable showers in a brown tent and let them run a few hours each day. In line I meet Aaron, a middle-aged Jew who bakes for my favourite Italian bakery. As we talk he *unconsciously* rubbed his belly, chest and pubis, and by that I understood that he was straight. During the shower a man and I were each other's mirror for shaving, tenderly pivoting a head, running a finger below the ear, along the jaw. Strange to be without a name, ID *and* mirror. The water is so gummy that shampood hair looks inorganic and black crud comes off it on a comb. When I think of my face I recall a random collection of features located in a photo or mirror; meaning falls away and I don't get a sense of why I look the way I do.

After dinner: In one corner of the tent an impromptu dance with conga drums made from empty water containers. Men in underwear gyrate. A flute joins in – lots of Bible shouts – *halleujah* and *amen* – a camp meeting cross-circuit of anger, sex, goodwill and frustration. Collective life has lost its charm. I miss women. I want to disappear into a book (as in childhood?) and reappear when I'm free (an adult?). I'm hostile and overfocused. As an act of aggression I shut my eyes and mentally locate and undress all the men who attract me; they eagerly submit or I overwhelm them with superhuman tenderness.

Saturday: Tomorrow is Gay Freedom Day and Enola Gay has called for our own Freedom Day Parade. Most men here are gentle so we never knew who was gay. Still, the men who attended our parade meeting were news to me. A farmer from Petaluma looked *exactly* like a farmer from Petaluma, etc. I take a lesson from the straight men and touch people more. During a meeting I let my head fall on John's shoulder. I channel my erotic life into brotherly hugs which appease my loneliness and give me ballast.

Saturday night: The posts creak, a windstorm – dilated eyes, a tremulous excitement in the spine – the tent pulses and heaves, we're inside a giant termite queen. Paul and I: both have lovers, both couples are monogamous *so far*, haven't slept with anyone else *yet*...

Sunday: Gay Freedom Day. We stuff clothes to make Mr Santa Rita and carry him on a sheet. Paul and others turn sheets into togas, shouting 'Toga! Toga!' We have noise makers and a man in a white wedding dress! We have chants: *Apples, Pears, Peaches and Cukes, We Are Fruits Who Don't Like Nukes.* We are nervous because 1) gay men have some problems with rape and murder in jail (you have to trust the system enough to put yourself in it) and 2) what if only ten people show up? But: 300 join us.

One group dresses in chief bikinis, another turns sheets and blankets into wimples and habits: Sisters of Perpetual Incarceration. We conclude at the loading platform with a talent show. The audience shouts, '*You too*, can be *sucked off*, in the Tornado that Dare Not Speak Its Name.' Affinity group structure enables political life to accept our differences so in this action I don't stop being a gay man.

Monday: The captain says, 'This is not Camp Friendly or Camp Sunshine'. New rules: single file lines; no wearing sheets; no tampons – the women had a parade too – or cups used as decoration; only 'Discreet Homosexual Activities' – in a tent of 400? We speculate they mean the men's movement men; they are mostly straight but touch each other intensely.

The legal team shake their heads, the judge won't compromise, we are sober. Guards roam around at night shining flashlights in our faces – I struggle in with the dawn.

I was in line for allergy pills for dust. The sergeant shouts, 'Circle, circle!' (imitating us?) and guards surround me.

Sergeant:	Maybe we should throw this one out?
Me *(my voice is too high)*:	Fine with me.
Sergeant:	Naw, he's too small a fish. *(then, confidentially)* Have you ever considered that this might be a dream, that you are asleep, alone,

and all this *(a wave of his arm at the tent)* is a figment of your imagination?

The true answer is, Yes – frequently. Eight days and I'm still in jail: the constant din surrounded by silence, the uncertainty, the cold nights, the food...

Me *(defensive)*:	Have you been watching too many *Twilight Zones*?
The guards:	Disrespect! Disrespect!

Here's one of my imaginary conversations with Judge Lewis:

Me:	As the days pile up we become more certain that we are political prisoners. We are punished for what we believe rather than for what we did. If we get nine days, $450 and two years probation for stopping traffic, how do you treat shoplifters – the guillotine?
Lewis *(rumour has him running for State Senate next year)*:	Face to face with a criminal, you don't negotiate a settlement. Our weapons defend a free country. Doubtless you would be happier in a totalitarian one.
Me:	With due respect, the same observation has been made about this court.

Tuesday: Paul leaves; he is flying to Kansas to help his parents harvest the wheat. I'm getting shell-shocked; I find I start crying when I imagine that I'm crying at home or crying in a restaurant (food) with Denny (love); that is I cry in anticipation. We're exhausted – faces either too slack or too focused, incomplete gestures, anxiety sharpened by the legal muddle. We are determined and angry and our physical number remains the most effective bargaining chip. Still, when people go to arraignment we give them a warm farewell.

I'm wearing a blue kerchief across my face like a bandit to combat the dust – it startles people; it completes my lack of identification. Half of us have a sore throat, sore lungs. I imagine Denny is angry at me.

The final chapter on the men's movement men: today one of them called me Sir and I enjoyed that respect.

Dinner taxed the imagination – nouvelle portions of cubed spam suspended in canned apple pie filling minus the apples, with a can of fruit cocktail thrown in, then warmed to the temperature of mucus and served with a slice of bread. We talked about Linzertorte. Before dinner the sergeant announced a new rule: if anyone throws food at the guards no one will eat. He was right to be nervous. We are giddy and depressed. Richard said, 'It's bureaucratic food, food in the abstract for abstract people.' We named the dish 'The Martyrdom of Saint Cecilia'. Many are constipated; mine is the opposite problem. The food ransacks my body: I have diarrhea every morning, just one blurt, like Fuck You.

The dust is a haze – people appear distant. It may contain asbestos.

Wednesday: Judge Lewis offered a $500 fine, but *finally* no probation. We meet to discuss the fine. I join the circle and the men look up for a second, big eyes, heads hardly moving. We sit on the dirt. I'm having a crisis of Pessimism of the Intellect. We wrangle for hours, we are indignant and spaced-out. Finally someone tells us (can it be true?) that the women quickly agreed on this message to Lewis: Shove it up your ass.

Night: Someone had an epileptic seizure out by the telephones. The guards made us carry him in a cot to the medical trailer – no doctor. When he started coming out of it, the guards rushed over, jumped him, applied hammerlocks, pushed pressure points, *handcuffed him*, then dragged him away screaming. Encounters with the guards are always inconclusive, except for this conclusion. They were like a sharp knife – so quick and professional we didn't feel scared until later.

Sometimes, just after lights out, the whole 400 fakes an orgasm in response to the 'Discreet Homosexual Activity' rule: ugh! ugh! ugh! oh! oh! oh! Someone shouts out in the darkness: 'How many erections have you had?' Shouted replies: 'I've only had two.' 'I've had four.' Then a murmur of 'Night, John. Night, John.'

Thursday: Dawn, the generators click off. Lots of us wake up from the sudden lack of noise. We lie awake in the cold.

Later: A new offer by the DA was upped by Lewis: Now it's time served plus five more days or $240. *Finally* there's no tactical advantage to stay here any longer. Our solidarity killed the two years probation, reduced the fine from $500 to $240, extracted a promise of equal sentencing; they are prepared to keep us here through the July 4th weekend. About 150 leave; more will leave tomorrow; hugs and applause from those who remain.

We are fingerprinted, photographed. I'm arraigned in a classroom with about twenty others. Still no ID's. They must accept the faces and the facts we provide. But we are precise – 'I've lived at x for eleven months, three weeks' – as though there are eyes everywhere. At 9.00pm I find myself on the outskirts of Livermore near MacDonald's twin arches.

At home: 11.30pm. Denny and I embrace, look at each other. I still have sea legs, I don't see why rooms aren't noisy and swaying. Harold brings over some Linzertorte for Enola Gay. We eat soberly.

At dawn I get up – coughing, worried. I vomit quietly and climb back in bed. Denny says, 'Why are you awake?' – a grievance in his voice. 'We prisoners get up early.' Denny asks if I'm okay. I say no and start crying. I cry for half an hour or so. I'm not sad – mostly stressed out. Finally he just rocks me. Do that, I say to him mentally.

In the morning, talking about the action, Denny says, 'It was a big deal and not a big deal'. That's right. It was a lot for me to do; I almost never felt in danger; I lost weight; I'm proud of myself; the world still doesn't stand much of a chance; it was important; I'll do it again.

Questions and Answers, and Two Vignettes

Aileen La Tourette

Introduction

'Questions and Answers' is an excerpt from *Nuns and Mothers*, a novel. Georgie and Helena have been lovers for some five years. They met and fell in love while still at school. Helena has had one other affair with a woman, is married, has two kids, lives in England and in conflict. Georgia is a high-powered career woman in a business world which demands that she conform, which she does except for her visits to Helena. She lives in the US. They are both American. In the excerpt, Georgia has just asked Helena why she ever married Jonathan in the first place. Helena answers her facetiously, but Georgia demands more.

Eventually Helena will come to the conclusion that she must leave both Jonathan and Georgia in order to live at peace with herself and affirm herself as a lesbian. At this point, though, the conflict is still raging.

The other two pieces are attempts to describe the paradoxical nature of my own initiation into womanhood. Paradoxical because it – the initiation – took place at the hands of women and was meant to prepare me for the hands of men. It did not. Both riding and dancing were activities engaged in at the very outset of adolescence, and they both gave strong and disturbing hints of an ability to respond physically which was not entirely in my control – the horseback riding experience – and an inability to respond which was equally outside my will – the impossibility of becoming the ultra-feminine ballerina I aspired towards.

*

Two Vignettes: Lessons

She had a wooden leg. Otherwise, she looked like an ageing Katherine Hepburn, burnt deep desert red. She walked with a profound, strenuous limp.

There was a husband. He had a nice, wide smile. The rest of him seems to have been invisible to me, at ten, like the Cheshire Cat permanently reduced to teeth. Certainly my Wonderland ended with the stable and the little ring her ponies circled. It didn't extend to the ordinary house or the ordinary husband.

Her housewifely, or horsewifely, duties were the mucking out of stalls and the currying of three ponies. Roger, fourteen hands high, was her mount. She had to press a spring in the wooden leg to make it bend before she climbed up onto his back. Once mounted, she and Roger were one. His hair was the same flame-coloured auburn as hers.

I was all right on horseback. At a walk. The first two lessons were slow and smooth, dream-paced. In my personal continuation of those dreams, Roger walked delicately over the high jumps in international competitions, while I sat dignified, unsmiling, elongated by the ironing out of time to a tall, willowy horsewoman instead of the pudgy pre-adolescent I was.

The third lesson ran at the wrong speed. Roger took off on a trot, at the instructions of my reluctant heels, and I was left behind, walking in dreamland.

'Go on,' she said patiently, my rose-coloured teacher. 'Up and down. Feel the rhythm of the horse's movements and follow it.'

Simple enough. Only there was no connection between me and my groin, or hips, or thighs. I existed from the knees down and the neck up, with occasional currents of life through the arms. If she had a wooden leg, I had a wooden torso. I sat in that saddle smiling fiercely, like a ship's figurehead. If arrows had gouged my chest like Saint Sebastian's, someone would have had to inform the head, as next of kin.

I arrived every week in the riding regalia I had received as a birthday present. Jodhpurs, boots, tweed hacking jacket, black velvet hat; and all I could do was walk. And smile.

On this particular day, she, too, seemed dejected, seemed even to share a little of my absurdity. What was she doing in a quiet New Jersey suburb, a red woman with a wooden leg, squaw and totem at once?

'I'm doing accounts today,' she said moodily. Her limp seemed deeper, her face drawn. Even her bristling electric hair, forever escaping its bun, seemed dun-coloured and dispirited. Her teeth looked horsey as she tried a smile.

Who'd said her teeth were horsey? My mother, jealous of a mana and magic with which she couldn't compete? Someone. Maybe they were right. Whoever it was couldn't bear to let anything escape the nervous, sawing little teeth of suburban judgement. Maybe nothing did escape.

She'd made me heave myself up on Roger's bare back, as if she couldn't be bothered to saddle him.

'Do anything you want,' she said with a horsey yawn. 'Trot, canter;

gallop if you get the urge. Set the jumps up if you feel like it.' She shrugged and disappeared into the unimaginable house.

Maybe she sat at a cherrywood desk and smoked cigars. Maybe the house was wood-panelled throughout, the rooms like stalls. Maybe her kitchen smelled of dung and hay. I would never find out. I was too terrified.

Meanwhile I was in pain. Roger's bare backbone bit right into that part of me for which I had no name. Once I thought 'body' was its name, and blushed whenever I heard the word. I was practically as red as she was, till someone explained. Since then it had been nameless. It was still nameless but it had sensation, all right.

The only way to relieve the pain, which I literally stumbled upon, was to have Roger clip along at a trot and then to rise and sit down again, delicately, barely touching him, to the rhythm of his heels. You had to skip a beat; that was what had confused me before. Once you got it, you got it.

I didn't think. There was no bone-weary, compassionate voice to encourage me. My pelvis rose and fell, my 'crotch' as we called it, if it was called anything. A crutch was something made of wood, that you walked with.

I didn't even notice when she reappeared, by the fence, smiling less like a horse than a seraph. I hardly dared smile back. I couldn't focus myself into more than one part of my body at once, and my crotch was already smiling.

'Keep going,' she shouted, giving me the victory 'V' as a symbol, perhaps, of what I'd discovered. Then she withdrew and I went round and round, dizzily, half-afraid to stop, half-carried away by an equestrian equivalent rapture of the deep. It began to get dark and two figures appeared by the fence, hers and my mother's.

'Right,' my teacher shouted. 'You can take him in and give him a good rub.'

She understood I needed time to prise myself loose, to turn human again from centauress. I felt more mermaid as I flopped to the ground and hobbled up to the barn. My hand travelling rhythmically over Roger's coat with the currycomb, I inhaled the intense, beloved odours of the barn, equally aware of the trees outside, the green smell, the gathering dark.

My revel ended, I had to climb into the car and become a little girl again, sleepy and grumpy with ordinariness, finding her landlegs again. Dealing with my mother's percipient jealousy, hot on my trail, resentful, piqued, eager to anchor me. Yet I would not have had it at all, had she not driven me the six or seven miles to and from the stable every week. When the riding school moved to greener pastures, lock stock and barrel, teacher, ponies, Cheshire husband, she sat by my bed as I sobbed, and sighed over me.

'Maybe you should go back to ballet,' she finally said, drily, and that made me laugh. But I did.

You can't be as exposed in the outdoors as you can indoors. Being clumsy and hopeless on the back of a pony, alone with my teacher for the most part, though occasionally a few other little girls would sit the smaller ponies, simply doesn't have the potential for humiliation as standing at a barre in a deserted church with ten or twelve others, all leotarded but none quite as uncomfortably bulky as yourself. Those who were fat weren't tall, and vice versa. Those who were fat or tall or otherwise malformed didn't have conical, precocious breasts that flopped inside their leotards. Breasts flopped, belly flopped, I flopped.

Yvonne taught ballet. She was short and neat and firm, and when she grabbed my hand to lead me away from the meagre shelter of the barre into the centre of the room, there to correct and chastise and generally insult me, her cigarette stung my palm. Riding had had its bad moments, but ballet was a masochist's delight.

Yvonne hid me in the back row at recitals. I slumped, shoulders rounding nicely to try and hide those mudpie-mounds on my chest. I projected myself into the sylphlike form of Mary Bourgholtzer, whose arms and legs had to be rubbed down with Milk of Magnesia to give her the desired pallor as she danced the North Wind. I didn't care. Even a Milk of Magnesia complexion couldn't detract from her romance. She was everything I wanted to be and wasn't, pallor and all; I was red-faced under spotlights and make-up, and looked like an unhealthy, harried, miniature businessman in a leotard with pointy, falsie-looking breasts.Everyone in the world thought my bust was foam rubber. They were so sure, they half-convinced me; but it wouldn't come off. And the money I won betting it was real was no consolation at all.

Mary Bourgholtzer didn't look like a ten-year-old transvestite Willy Loman. She looked lke a ten-year-old North Wind. She had breasts that rose subtly and proudly, unmistakeably real. One pink satin-toe shoe shook loose during her longest solo and she kicked it contemptuously away, out from under the dark blue net of her tutu. She was icy and complete. She remained regal the time she spent the night with me and we flashed each other peeks of our pubic hair under her green silky scarf. She wore silky scarves knotted cowgirl style around her neck, which exoticized our school uniform unbelievably; after that, they eroticized it unbelievably.

Yvonne gave me one hell of a swan song. After my woeful comeback, she made me work up to a reasonable standard. Then she created a part for me in the next recital.

It was an interpolated Coppelia, and I was a school superintendent. I had to examine a huge pair of scissors, frowningly, stomp and storm around the stage in trousers, tails and top hat. She had picked up on my businessman potential. My one and only appearance as a ballerina was made in drag.

Come the night and the dramatic, forbidding music, and I sent a rapidly prayed 'Here goes nothing' to a friendly devil and threw myself into it, menacing authoritarian disciplinarian – schoolgirl. I loved it.

'So,' Yvonne said to me afterwards. She came from somewhere else, of course, could not have sprung from boring New Jersey, could not have spoken with a bubblegum twang or a pregnant-mosquito whine. 'You enjoy yourself, eh?' She grinned and patted me on the shoulder.

*

Questions and Answers

'That's a great little stand-up comedy routine you've got there,' Georgia, my lover, says firmly. 'But I didn't want a comedy act. I wanted an answer to my question. I wanted to know why you married Jonathan.'

'I can't say like Everest, because he was there,' I recognize a familiar weakness in my voice, inspired by just this familiar question. 'Because he wasn't there. I had to pursue him across the ocean and then chase him all over London.'

'So we've eliminated that one,' she says pleasantly, my interrogator. 'Could it be that you loved him?'

Could it? Easy to say yes. Easy to say no. Hard to fend off the tidal wave of emotion that roars up like a million white stallions – white stallions? – tails and manes like wave-spume and sweat and tears. And blood. Hard to avoid those heels.

Jonathan.

'We met by a map outside Blackwell's in Oxford.' I want, suddenly, to plot our course like a general planning a war, to plant pins with coloured heads on the important battle-sites. 'I think I wanted him – sexually – right away. Only I didn't recognize the feeling.'

'Being a virgin.'

'Being a virgin.' I had wanted her first, and not recognized that feeling either. Being a virgin. The dangling participles around here are getting to me. But I feel I must go blindly plunging on, not backtrack. 'I went on wanting him but it changed. The wanting. Less about wanting to incorporate something in him I recognized as my birthright, but thought I wouldn't have, or was too cowardly to go and get for myself –'

'Like ambition and energy –'

'– like ambition and energy – it changed into just wanting him. Wanting him to give himself to me. Because –' I want to describe him, as he stood by that map, but I can't. Silvery-black curly hair stuck out from his face in a sort of Jewish Afro; only there were no Afros yet. The same christmas-tree stuff bubbled up on his chest where his red wool shirt was open. His eyes were elusive grey-green chameleon, similar to hers. Would that make it better, or worse, for her?

'Because he was the most beautiful man I'd ever seen. He answered some hunger in me the way certain landscapes answered me, the first time I saw them. The landscapes are rocky and harsh and sunburnt. Greece and Spain. I'd give all the leafy green foliage in the world for a parched, scorched, threadbare landscape. I didn't know that till I went there. Like with him. Is that love?' I shrug. 'I fell in love with what I thought was him. What I thought his landscape meant. I made it up and called it Jonathan, that meaning. I'd never found him. I know less about him than I know about people I've known for half an hour. I've never had him, either.'

'What?'

'I mean – he likes games with sex. Teasing is his speciality.'

'There's a lot to be said for teasing,' she says, teasingly.

'Sure there is. It's very exciting. Very heating. But it isn't enough. Once in a while, when we make love in the much-maligned missionary position, I have the feeling he almost – almost – gives himself. But he draws back from the brink.' Oh, shit. There's a lump in my throat the size of a baseball. 'But I get confused about what's him and what's men. He's been the only one, really. He cuts me off all the time, and I don't know,' a weird convulsive sound punctuates the sentence, shocking us both, 'I don't know if that's just the nature of the beast, or him. He just cuts me off. Talking. Making love. Being together. I feel he gets his bit – as much as he wants, or needs – then it's over, and I'm still in the middle, or even at the beginning. Even if I've come, as far as sex goes. You know?'

She nods.

'And I do come. Almost infallibly. But I make it happen. I sit on top of him and make it happen. Sometimes I hate it like that, I feel like I'm using him – but he doesn't mind. He prefers it, I think; he doesn't have to do much. It never seems to occur to him I might want more than just any old orgasm. His tenderness is locked down deep, and it's so rare it seems rich when he produces it, but I've come to the conclusion it only seems rich because of its rarity. And I think he values it that way. He's afraid – God, he's afraid! – he's afraid that if he let it be common currency it'd be devalued, somehow. He thinks it has to be special or it's – unworthy.'

'So,' she clears her throat, 'he devalues yours. Assuming you show it rather more often.'

'I used to. And then, he did. He didn't answer me –' I smile. 'He did what I did when you first asked me that question. He entertained me instead. Now he doesn't bother. It's hardly surprising, given – everything.'

Meaning, her.

'What're you waiting for?'

'He just deflects me, nowadays. I guess I'm waiting till the deflection becomes rejection. Then I can, as they say, go in peace.'

'But –'

'I know, I know. But I can't seem to give up. I try. I should. He holds me back. He ties me in knots. He gives me just enough rope to hang myself and I do, every time. But I keep thinking it'll all change.'

'Ah.'

'Yes. I keep thinking the next time I turn around he'll be there. Then he is, and it's great – for ten minutes. Then I feel like shit.'

'Ten minutes?'

'The first ten minutes. Or hour. Or whatever. Then he has to go, or he starts to think about when he has to go, and it all collapses, he isn't really there at all. And when he goes it feels like an amputation. Of love. Of *me*. So I go around feeling amputated, then I recover, and by then he's back and it starts all over again. And that, Georgia, is the clearest way I can describe our relationship.'

'I'm sorry I asked.'

A Grossly Overrated Problem

Codes of Conduct

Noël Greig

Schizophrenia (n). Mental disorder known as 'split personality', characterised by asocial behaviour, introversion, and a loss of touch with one's environment.

(Collins Shorter English Dictionary)

A Dream

Sitting on a great expanse of blue carpet is a tiny child. Naked as the day he was born, gazing around him, unclenching his fists. I'm looking down at him. In my hand I hold a string of red glass beads, threaded onto cotton. I cross to the baby, squat and hold out a finger to the child. The child refuses to take hold of it. I touch the child's head gently. The child pulls away, screwing up his eyes. I offer him the string of glass beads. He hits out at them angrily. I gently hang the beads over one tiny wrist. The child shakes them off as if they burn. I hold them out again, close to the child's face. A chubby hand closes around the gift. I smile. The child begins to tear the string of beads apart with its tiny fingers. Breaks the cotton and scatters the red stones across the floor. The child does not like me. A door opens and a women enters. It is my mother. She crosses to the child, picks him up in her arms and whispers to him 'Come along Noël, it's time for bed.' She carries him out of the room and closes the door, leaving me sitting on the blue carpet with the red beads scattered around me.

*

I grew up queer in a normal world. I have tried to change queer in its application to my sexuality, and writing about it has been part of that attempt. But that dream (had in more recent times when queer had been rejected for gay) was a reminder that no amount of words on paper will dissolve that feeling of dislocation, of secret selves at war inside my skin. I once thought experience was sequential and that we skipped from one part of life to the next like this year's fashion in clothes, but of course that is a foolish idea. I will always be growing up queer and dreams frequently confirm this. Perhaps writing can help though, a way of pinning down the feelings, Naming the Fears. Words written and (hopefully) words heard or read can make a sort of map. The map will not make the forest full of demons disappear, but with its help we can recognise the dangerous paths.

Schizophrenia

For a number of years, whenever thoughts of childhood and adolescence surfaced, an insistent little phrase would rattle round my head like a dried pea in a can. It went: 'They would call it growing up but I call it schizophrenia,' and it caught, pretty well, the keynote of my existence during that time of my life.

I remember one Sunday, sometime in the mid-fifties, when I had, as usual, sneaked the weekly Muck-Rakers up to my room before my parents woke. On that occasion I came across a long article with the title 'The Twilight Men', plus pictures of a male (in silhouette and mac) in a park, at dusk, gazing towards a group of young boys. A face we could not see, but a mind seething with filthy lusts, we were told. From that moment, with a shock of recognition, I was able to identify my own desires, until then simply vague moods and imaginings washing around inside me. The vocabulary of that article gave me the means to place myself in the world and the tone of it left me in no uncertain doubt that I had better keep my mouth closed. For about a year after, it was the vogue at school for the boys to point fingers at less-than-manly pupils and unmarried masters and whisper 'he's a Twilight'. So that's what I was, though I was not about to let them know it, and I entered that period of – schizophrenia.

I call it schizophrenia in the loose popular sense of contrasting patterns of behaviour alternating violently. My alternations were not visibly violent – the patterns were mental rather than manifested. Yet, as I'll explain, the struggle between the two versions of 'me' was bloody and violent. A strictly medical academic (male?) mind would probably chide me for sloppy use of a particular word, and indeed I wish we could invent a word for the particular gay experience I'm talking about. We haven't, so I use their jagged word for it because its very sound zooms in on the jagged feelings their world imposed on me.

From then on, of a morning, two people would look in the bathroom mirror, get into the same suit of school clothes. There was the bright Grammar School pupil, marked down for university one day, popular with the girls, and there was the boy who desperately wanted to kiss his best friend or be fucked by the history master. The former self, in order to bar the latter from making his presence known, began to develop a set of procedures; an elaborate, sophisticated code of conduct, the prime rule of which was *Check Everything*.Looks and glances had to be carefully monitored – don't allow eyes to linger on a boy too long, don't gaze at the history master, *never* look at a male any lower than the waist. Stance and posture had to be under a constant review – no hint of droop, limpness, don't let those hips swing! Voice of course was crucial – no giggles, no high-pitched tones etc. Facial muscles had to be in control – if the words 'queer' or 'Twilight' came up, no twitch should betray lack of composure. Clothes and the manner they were worn should not indicate 'fussiness'. Conversation had to be moulded – make it big, authoritative, swear more than most. This and much more was the order of the day, and not just an on/off job, it was a full time preoccupation, the motor of life.

Now came the really difficult part. Having constructed code Number One, there was code Number Two to deal with. The hidden, invisible person, though so carefully screened from the world, was still there. What's more, in my case (and I know now, in the case of many of my gay friends) there was the feeling that this 'other' was really All Right. Don't ask me where that feeling came from, I couldn't for the life of me say, but there it was. Then it was hidden away, with its hideous names, but one day, I knew, this person would want to breathe freely and had to be allowed some space in adolescent life. And so double-double code Number Two.

Example: sitting in the coffee-bar with your 'girlfriend' and your 'best friend', you sit, arms around her, deep in conversation with him (careful not to look too deeply into his eyes – he's sitting next to you anyway, all three on the same seat, you in the middle, so you don't have to look straight at him, thank goodness). But he's got his arm over the back of the seat. You're wearing a T-shirt, and for a moment, his hand touches the back of your neck. By accident, of course, and barely touching, but you can feel the flesh. Code One says 'withdraw at once or/and make a pouff joke', but Code Two says 'it's OK, keep cool, he can't see what you're thinking, enjoy the thrill'. Fear and desire fight, desire wins a few moments for itself and in that half-minute you have achieved something tangible – all the fantasies of love and lust, sex and romance, sensuality and friendship *do* have a relation to actual, social, physical life. So Code Two is about seeking for those times when Code One can be relaxed. That's a full-time job as well.

The thing to do I discovered, was to beat them at their own game in subtler ways than acting big and swearing more. It was to gain a purchase in the male world of achievement. With the kudos that came with winning cups for running and swimming (thus side-stepping the problem of hated group sports), putting on the end-of-term plays, getting the best exam results, it was possible to win male admiration and respect. This provided a margin of camaraderie, not dependent upon the sexist pack-hunting of young women, in which Code One could soften at the edges: you're in a stronger position to admit, yes, you actually like poetry, if you've won the half-mile on Sports Day. I tell you getting really good at history was just as much about visiting the history master at his own home on a weekend as loving the subject. (Alas we only talked.) Such was the success of my tactics, that by the end of the sixth form, I'd integrated various bits of myself so well that the tearaway who was clever and won things could actually play a dandy in some stage production and get away with it. Could even begin to write mooncalf poems about other boys (never shown, of course, to a soul). Yet it was still the fight inside and the world was still a minefield, and I knew I wasn't honest (not to the 'girlfriend', who was being cheated rotten, or to the 'best friend' – who might have had the same feelings as myself).

Undeniably it was exciting at times, and such habits of behaviour have left their mark on those men who feel that life was more exciting before Gay Liberation robbed them of the bitter-sweet romance of being 'naughty boys'. Yet it was not good. It is a wrong sort of world where young people have to learn habits of slyness and deceit in order to survive. 'Coming Out' is, I think, just a start. Not merely in the process of linking sexuality with the outer world of politics and relationships, but in the constant awareness of the shadowy battle that took place between the two personalities in the same suit. I believe that childhood is, for all of us, female and male, gay and heterosexual, of whatever creed and colour, a process of subterfuge, where often habits can be learnt that can damage for life; the person with homosexual desires can experience that in a particular, focused way.

Funnily enough, it's often at this point that good-thinking heterosexual friends stick. Prepared as they are to support and listen, change their behaviour and language vis-à-vis lesbians and gays, the homoeroticism of childhood pulls them dead in their tracks. When, on being presented with 'the children' I have said something like 'I hope the gay ones don't have to hide it at school as much as I did,' the look of panic on the face of the proud parent is a picture indeed. Whose childhood are they denying, their offspring's or their own? What childhood coding system of their own haven't they faced up to? What other selves put down and battled with?

Finally, the phrase rattling round my head came out as a song lyric. It goes like this:

They call it growing up but I call it schizophrenia
They call it being alive but I call it schizophrenia

They drive a wedge between your body and your mind
They've got you caught up in the original double-bind

They say you're acting strange, you've been acting all your life
In a play you haven't written, in a script that's based on lies

They say it isn't right for a man to love a man
And a woman in a woman's arms is upsetting the natural plan

They so confuse your mind they make you hate yourself
And when they've filled you full of madness they say they want
   to help

They call it growing up but I call it schizophrenia
They call it being alive but I call it schizophrenia.

Writing this song, standing on stages and singing it sometimes, was
part of making the map through the forest.
   The dreams still occur.

Part of this essay was originally published in *Achilles Heel* No. 6/7.

The Tables Need Turning

Jan Parker

The idea that heterosexuality is of itself oppressive to women and tailored to men's needs and interests is not new in circles familiar with feminist debate and, some may say, not particularly controversial either. The idea of 'compulsory heterosexuality' is newer and makes many more hackles rise. Despite the fact that compulsory heterosexuality was named as one of the 'crimes against women' by the Brussels Tribunal on Crimes Against Women in 1976 – one of the first 'official' acknowledgements of its existence that has since been joined by others – it is still mostly dismissed as a loony idea. Yet many features of oppression that have been attributed to sexism are attributable to heterosexism. This may be hard even for some feminists to swallow, but the idea is gaining ground and in this lies a direction that needs pursuing.

This book, called *Heterosexuality* and written by lesbians and gay men, is further evidence that an important shift in focus is slowly happening. It is far more pertinent and clarifying for questions – and the finger – to be pointed at heterosexuality than at lesbianism and homosexuality. The effort of finding and defining our identity and then surviving is a long slog, so it's not surprising that a lot of lesbian and gay energy has gone into this. We're forced into, at best, a corner; and at worst, the closet (cells, psychiatric units). We've been so pathologised that it's still hard to break out of their image of us however much one's guts reject this pressure. We can break through this block by demanding that heterosexuals explain their sexuality rather than accept being forced to constantly explain ours to them.

Heterosexuality is a subject it's difficult not to be knowledgeable about. We're bombarded by it, with information about how heterosexuals should and do behave towards their own and the other gender. From a lesbian viewpoint heterosexuality often strikes me as peculiar, if not downright weird, these days. It's easy to feel like an anthropologist spending an evening in the local pub – watching the heterosexual signals, the codes of behaviour and appearance – and to let my mind dwell on the rituals involved, the most obvious example and glaring symbol of institutionalisation being the wedding, with all the fantastic hetiquette and paraphernalia that the occasion conjurs. There's a minefield of material waiting for anthropologists who don't want to go abroad. There's no way that all this heterosexual palaver is 'natural' and 'normal', as its participants are convinced it is. If I stuck rigidly to my convictions I would devote this chapter to some sort of 'behavioural study'. When I thought about heterosexuality, however, what struck me most was how my attitude towards it has changed since I became a lesbian and through my lesbian experience of ten years. Several episodes came to mind.

I remember very well the day I read Adrienne Rich's pamphlet *Compulsory Heterosexuality and Lesbian Existence*. After several years' engagement with lesbian politics it was one of those days when the clouds lifted and the light shone more strongly. I was deeply impressed and was an immediate, albeit easily won, convert. Her idea that heterosexuality is a system, a political institution that is imposed, managed, organised, propagandised and maintained by force is not a purely rhetorical case; it is researched, strongly argued and sensitively written. Aspects of male power that feminists have seen as 'only' producing sexual inequality, Rich interpreted as specifically enforcing heterosexuality. In short, it made me feel like a hyperactive fruit machine: lots of pennies fell into place. Though these ideas are the core of my thinking now, they're not widely available ones. Most heterosexuals don't see their sexuality as constructed and organised in very detailed ways, but simply as the way they are, the way the world is. It's a 'personal' and 'private' matter, not a political one in any way and terms such as 'sexual preference' are used in order to 'explain' it all. Those who don't fit in are seen as victims of deviancy who must explain, justify and defend themselves. One reason why I welcome a shift in focus that turns the tables of discussion is that I remember that frame of mind well. Rich, where were you in 1975?

Eleven years ago I had my first lesbian relationship. Ten years ago I 'became a lesbian' and soon after this 'came out'. In between and – significantly – before an involvement with the women's movement, I put myself and especially my brain cells through the wringer. It's no coincidence that a lot of lesbian and gay writing has been about 'coming out'. First you have to feel good about being a lesbian yourself, then you have to prepare for the reaction and taking the world on. 'Why, why, why am I this way?' I asked myself. 'What's the cause, the explanation?' I felt very isolated. I read voraciously. Stopping work as a librarian (no helpful books to be found there, needless to say) and moving into the more liberal environment of a university sped up the process. I opted for a course called 'The Biological and Interpersonal Basis of Sex Differences' taught, as luck would have it, by a lesbian and feminist biologist who made sure that tackling heterosexual myths and prejudices was as integral a part of an anti-sexist approach as it should be. By the time I came out I was well equipped for arguments that I wouldn't bother with now and cringe to overhear. Heterosexuals would set the terms of discussion and I'd be able to witter away at length about hormones, genes, the animal kingdom, Sappho, Rome, the family and throw in the odd philosophical comment on human nature. As the task wore me down I began to develop one-off lines that were attempts to stop the conversation.

'What do you do in bed?'

'Sleep, read, talk, make love – what do you do?'

Such ploys were also an attempt to stop exposing myself to such scrutiny. These sorts of conversations are ridiculous but they still go on. It's difficult, impossible, not to feel resentment and anger that heterosexuals rarely, never, are subjected to this sort of questioning or have to explain themselves. Is it unreasonable, given Joe or Jill Public's general level of understanding, to stop engaging in these kind of discussions, answering often offensive questions? It may increase knowledge and 'understanding', but does it fundamentally change anything?

As I became more involved in Left, and especially feminist political activity, my tack slowly began to change. When the 'Sex Differences' course was run the next year, right-wing scientists took over the lectures and began teaching-preaching misogyny, homophobia and anti-lesbianism. In response the student women's group, gay society and Communist Party demanded control of three lectures and, to our amazement, succeeded. I never saw a fuller lecture hall in my whole time at university. It was packed with attentive and potentially sympathetic students. From the organisers' point of view things didn't run so smoothly. A lesbian (me) and a gay man (who was a neighbour and friend) were to address one of the lectures. We couldn't agree on a common approach, to the extent that we had a huge argument about it. 'Don't put their backs up,' he said, 'we don't get this sort of chance very often.' I pulled out and sat in the audience. Off he went, talking about his family background, how he came to terms with being gay and how good he felt about it, what sort of relationships he had. Most people looked convinced that he wasn't a bogeyman or a threat to the campus. It was a congenial atmosphere and it all seemed very easy for them. The moment one lesbian, echoed by another, chipped in with how we saw our sexuality as also political discomfort set in and the attacks began. The whole issue had been viewed purely as a question of who went to bed with whom and what did politics have to do with that? We however were seen as feminist crusaders who weren't really interested in pleasure and as perverts who were merely trying to justify politically our sexual desires. What strikes me now is that we were still only saying that lesbianism was political; not that heterosexuality was political too. It was a revealing incident and left me thinking, as always, that there was more homework to be done.

The idea of 'political lesbianism' was not a new one, in that it had been fermenting in America since the early 1970s. It burst into profile in a big way in Britain in 1979 when the Leeds Revolutionary Feminist group wrote a conference paper called 'Political Lesbianism: The Case Against Heterosexuality'.[1] When this was published in *WIRES* (the internal national newsletter of the women's movement) the debate raged, literally, for over a year. It caused a furore in the women's movement which was avidly followed by thousands. It shook things up and it changed lives. Many a guilty lesbian became a lesbian feminist and there were heterosexuals who became lesbians, as well as those who defensively stood their ground. The reaction was such that many are still recovering. This paper began to turn the tables and received a lot of criticism, much of which was anti-lesbian. It talked a lot about 'fucking', i.e. heterosexual penetration. Many saw the paper as an attack on heterosexual feminists rather than on heterosexuality and understood withdrawal of sexual services from men as the sum total of its strategy. One of its effects was to make heterosexual feminists feel guilty and very, very defensive. There has been so much more feminist debate about sexuality since this episode that it would be easy to forget its impact. It was the *beginning* of an analysis of how heterosexuality is central to women's oppression. It didn't explain *how* it worked but wordsmith Rich, bless her, did. It's all relative, but life's been easier since.

Despite the stereotype of lesbians, changing your sexual/political identity is not like changing your clothes or getting your hair cut. Most of us who are/have become lesbians have been through a difficult, complex and often painful process of change that doesn't suddenly stop. Often the nature of this process only becomes clear very gradually as time goes on. This race through my lesbian years traces how my attitude to heterosexuality has changed. I began as a 19-year-old with the attitude that most heterosexuals still hold, but I had to *fit in* to it as a lesbian. It was all about saying I was normal *too* and asking for tolerance, acceptance and peaceful coexistence. I fell straight into the hole dug by the heterosexual tactic of 'sexual preference' and also fell for the line that it's an *equal* choice between heterosexuality and lesbianism. But anything was then better than being an out-and-out pervert.

It goes without saying that I have no motivation to fit in any more. I prefer sanity. I know I'm still judged by heterosexuals but fortunately I take it as an irritant rather than a pressure to conform. I now want heterosexuals to hear the ideas of compulsory heterosexuality and make understanding *their* sexuality a priority. In her foreword Rich writes:

heterosexual feminists will draw political strength for change from taking a critical stance towards the system of coercion which demands heterosexuality; lesbians cannot assume we are untouched by that institution. There is nothing about such a critique that requires us to think of ourselves as victims, as having been brainwashed or totally powerless.[2]

I understand that it's not very helpful, in any situation, to have a 'victim' approach, but confess that I often find that easier said than done. I still have enough heterosexual friends to know that they're not Stepford Wife robots, but I still see a lot of Pavlovian women and men around. I find it hard not to see heterosexual women as a combination of oppressor (by virtue of their actions, attitudes and heterosexual 'privileges') and victims. The tables turn indeed.

I recall a scene in the film *The Killing of Sister George* when George and Childie arrange to meet heterosexual Mercy Croft at the Gateways, knowing Mercy would be unaware that it was a lesbian club. A friend once nicknamed Mercy 'the woman with the performing eyebrows' because of her reaction to all the sights before her; most peculiar if not disturbing. I rarely go to hetty rave-ups, but when a recent holiday occasioned an inquisitive visit, 'for a laugh', to a hetty tea dance on the sea front, I remembered Mercy. The cruising and behaviour were extraordinary. I did my best to keep my eyebrows under control and found it all fascinating and bizarre.

Many heterosexual feminists are offended by the notion that they are victims of compulsory heterosexuality. After all, doesn't it deny the principle that every woman's experience is valid and real and that women have the capacity and the right to make their own choices? I can do without listening to how good and different their man is, but don't think there's any harm in heterosexuals being under pressure to assert their happiness after we've been pushed into years of shouting almost banal slogans such as 'Glad to be Gay'. In the main, their offence at having their experiences denied is blinkered. If a woman is taking it on a purely personal level and is a woman who is familiar with the issues and debates, perhaps she has made a *real* choice (?) but this can hardly be said to be the situation for women in general. There's more to a choice than the simple awareness of an alternative. Heterosexuality is a coercive system and although ideology plays a huge role, it's by no means the only factor.

Lesbians and gay men are, by our existence, a resistance movement. Whilst I'm all for swelling the ranks, it's about time the idea that sleeping with our own sex is a revolutionary act that – on its own – reaps great changes, was knocked on the head. Some of my favourite lines are from Robin Morgan's poem 'Monster':

I want a woman's revolution like a lover,
I lust for it, I want so much this freedom,
this end to struggle and fear and lies
we all exhale, that I could die just
with the passionate uttering of that desire.[3]

It's ironic enough that Robin Morgan has returned to heterosexuality, has even married. A further irony is that most of us, especially gay men, continue to desire the lover but have stopped lusting for the revolution. Where are we going?

Compulsory heterosexuality is not a sexual civil rights sidekick doomed to remain on the bottom of the agenda. It is a fact of life, a major oppression. *That's* the way the world is and nobody except us is going repeatedly to assert this in these times. We've been arguing on heterosexuality's terms and barking up the wrong tree too often, too long. What's in a statistic for example? The line about us being 10 per cent of the population has had its tactical uses, one example being a way of justifying an appropriate (though it never is) allocation of resources from sympathetic Labour local government authorities. Going along with the arguments that see us as a fixed percentage of the population smacks of the genes and hormones routine to me and offers no progress in the long term. It deflects attention away from the amount of energy and force that is put into keeping the vast majority on the heterosexual track. It is what these practices are, how they operate and how they can be changed that we've got to concentrate on.

I don't mean by this that the current functions and activities of lesbians and gay men are insignificant at all. It's vital to have our own resources: centres, switchboards, publications, archives, police monitoring groups, and it's vital to have a culture: theatre, bars, clubs, exhibitions and so on. The impact of an uncloseted life forces us to confront a new, more whole, but still very difficult reality and all this helps isolation and survival and has an impact. But we have to go beyond our own needs and beyond civil rights.

'Out of the Closets' was the rallying cry of gay liberation, but it has proved to be inadequate as a total political statement or way of life for gay men and especially lesbians. Yet movement men are still flogging this horse, are still stuck in 1969. Denis Lemon wasted the opportunity of a 30-minute TV programme (*Diverse Reports*, 5 December 1984) and made a call to 'come out' his stunning conclusion after talking to several sacked gay employees and visiting Rugby Council, which had just officially banned employing lesbians and gay men by removing that horrible expression 'sexual orientation' from its equal opportunities policy. Brian Kennedy made the same mistake by concluding a feature in *City Limits* magazine (18 January 1985) with:

the single most effective way of contending the rampant prejudice and homophobia around is by 'coming out' to family and friends. Some may not like it, but at least they are meeting the real you and not the alien creature that they have been led to believe the homosexual is.

Encouraging people to put their neck on the line with an increasing likelihood of it being chopped off is not an adequate guide to action. It speaks volumes for the advancement of male gay theory. What chance do people have of finding the real you/me when there's such a retreat into conventionality and Victorian values going on?

The need to shift focus, turn the tables and talk about compulsory heterosexuality is becoming all the more urgent. The pressure to conform in a society that is becoming increasingly right-wing has become more intense. The Right's message to women is that we are the emotional and sexual property of men, and the institutions by which women are traditionally controlled are being strengthened by legislation, the media, censorship and many other means. We've no choice but to change tack and raise this issue if we want the resistance movement to strengthen rather than be forced underground.

1 Published, with the ensuing correspondence, as *Love Your Enemy? The debate between heterosexual feminism and political lesbianism* by Onlywomen Press, 1981.
2 *Compulsory Heterosexuality and Lesbian Experience* by Adrienne Rich. Foreword in reprint by Antelope Publications, USA. Available in Britain and published by Onlywomen Press.
  Both of the above available from Sisterwrite, 190 Upper Street, London N1; and hopefully most 'radical' bookshops at least.
3 'Monster' by Robin Morgan, from her first collection *Monster*, published by Random House, but restricted to the U.S. market owing to the legal controversy concerning the poem 'Arraignment'.

The Nature of Heterosexuality

Jon Ward

I have a grassy Scutcheon spy'd
Where Flora blazons all her pride

Andrew Marvell

No one can willingly give up the name of human

Edward Bond

The *nature* of . . . an expression that promises to grasp both the core and the totality of its subject. In fact, what follows is only a glance at this imponderable 'nature'. But why 'nature' at all? Because 'nature' appears at the crux of the sexual conflict. Because I write from a position that is deemed 'unnatural'. Because of the presumption, which gives point to my argument, that the nature of heterosexuality is 'nature' itself.

1   Social Constructs

There is a cast of mind, prevalent on the left of this debate, that would object: but heterosexuality has *no* nature. Here, 'nature' is taken to mean essence – the heart of the thing, its being as such. And the consensus to which I refer has set itself against essence in every guise.[1] This is the basis on which the term '*homo*sexuality' has been placed under suspicion. Homosexuality, so the theory runs, is an ersatz reality, talked into appearance over the past couple of centuries. The by-product of cultural fragmentation, intensified sexual discourse, shifting dialogues of power, homosexuality is the ephemeral brainchild of that Olympian artificer, 'social construction'.[2] People like myself imagined we had found homosexuality within us; now we learn that we have found ourselves within homosexuality. If we persevere in wearing this chimerical garment – 'I am gay' – it is in a strange twilight of actions without centres, a condition rich in strategies but empty of substance.

So much for homosexuality. Then, surely, the case against *hetero*sexuality goes harder. Indeed, the brief history has been summarily composed and dismissed: 'The invention of heterosexuality, 1892–1982'.[3] It isn't difficult to re-assemble the pathetic tale, and before proceeding to my own perspective, I shall sketch the picture of heterosexuality suggested by the prevailing climate of radical scepticism.

2   *Heterosexuality: A Potted History*

We know that the term 'heterosexuality' was coined in the annals of Victorian sexual science, where medicine was surveying, with obsessive diligence, the landscape of the perversions: necrophilia, coprophilia, bestiality, homosexuality . . . A touchstone was needed to mark the thoroughfare from which these bizarre enormities diverged. Hence 'heterosexuality'.

But the new category never acquired the status of a scientific object. It was merely a piece of equipment, an empty negative marking the horizon of the perversions. In itself, it exerted no fascination. No condition was discovered which could be diagnosed as 'heterosexual', no individual characteristic of the heterosexual species. When attention turned from the perversions to sexual normalcy, excitement lay in what distinguishes men and women in their desires, not what unites them.[4]

Beyond sexual science, the currency of the word 'heterosexual' is extremely recent – as recent as popular awareness of a self-conscious gay movement. When in the late 1960s, homosexuality, already unique among the perversions in manifesting a viable subculture, proclaimed for itself the legitimacy reserved for married love, the faithful needed to know where they stood. Decent 'heterosexual' people. In the presence of a public gay consciousness, men and women established a tactical unity under this tinny shelter. They created for themselves a novel singularity, a 'sexual identity' to maintain against the irritant of the homosexual protest. 'Heterosexuality', by this token, reveals itself not as an entity, but as a reflex, well characterised by the plaintive title of a recent American publication: *In Defense of Heterosexuality*.[5]

3   *Is This the Way to Think About It?*

'Homosexuality', 'heterosexuality': constructs without substance, labels without objects. That's the attitude, if not the conviction, which pervades much of the writing currently undertaken at the frontiers of the sexual struggle. A kind of historical nominalism has captured the field.[6] But is it the most productive way to think? The savage pleasures of deconstruction leave in their wake a cool vacancy. In this state – almost camp in its airy cynicism – everything falls as soon as it is named, and we feel ourselves uniquely protected from folly. We are not to be taken in! And yet – the mobility that should result has proved strangely elusive.

Mobility is certainly the aim. Jeffrey Weeks, a standard bearer in history's campaign against 'essence', proposes *radical pluralism*. It's a streetwise ethic, tactful, lenient, optimistic – but necessarily lacking in content. More than ethics, we need a wealth of expression. But work in this field is remarkable for its paucity. In Britain, the proponent of pluralism is almost alone among gay theorists in maintaining a steady flow of books.

The reduction of sexual identities by historical analysis produces a wisdom which is too easy to be useful. But the historicist tendency cannot be dismissed lightly. From where I write, as a gay man, it's virtually all there is. Feminist theory makes free with psychoanalysis and romantic biologism.[7] Both are questionable recourses, but they engender a valuable diversity. Gay thought, by contrast, having suffered humiliation at the hands of Freud, and having long since lost the cause of nature's 'third sex', now clings to history with a certain grimness.

For reasons I shall make clear, I do not believe that 'heterosexuality' can be understood without crossing the frontier of historical explanation. But first, the frontier must be reached. And this requires not a withdrawal, but a more extensive exploration of the historical terrain. 'Heterosexuality', a relatively trivial construction, is but the latest variation on a theme which stretches interminably through the preceding centuries. It is this theme – the *pre*-history of heterosexuality – which must be considered before the historical analysis can be said to be exhausted.

4   The Sexual Norm: A Larger History

Before 1892, there may have been no 'heterosexuality'; but that is not to say there was no norm – no conception, widely understood and widely embraced, of the sexual good. The pre-history of 'heterosexuality' is the genealogy of this norm.

Now it is well known, even in our own age of strident salvationists, that all norms tend towards silence. For every book that today defends the supremacy of heterosexuality, there are a thousand which assume it. The history of sexual virtue is no monotone, but neither is it incoherent. It is the narrative of a loaded silence.

Glancing back over the past two thousand years, we can identify a quality of paranoia giving shape to this silence. In the Christian era, erotic propriety is what remains after the diseases, corruptions, abominations and execrations of sexual misdemeanour have been vomited out by ecclesiastical piety. Key terms such as 'sodomite' and 'buggery' evolved throughout the Medieval and Renaissance periods, adopting and shedding associations – sin, disease, heresy, witchcraft, disorder. In doing so, they drew a moving outline around the sexual good. Despite a dramatic change of language and institutions, this process continued into the modern era. As they mapped the perversions, the sexologists of the late nineteenth and early twentieth centuries implicitly located and defined the small space in which legitimate sexuality found its domain.

The positive content of this domain yields itself only reluctantly. But there is one term which, by its almost casual recurrence in text after text, suggests a striking obduracy at the heart of sexual history. The term is 'nature'. It is 'nature' which trickles like an unimpeded stream through the vast narrative of sex. A few examples:

First century:

> For this cause, God gave them up unto vile affections: for even their women did change the natural use into that which is against nature; and likewise also the men, leaving the natural use of the woman, burned in their lust one toward another.
>
> St Paul[8]

Third century:

> To have sex for any other purpose than to produce children is to violate nature.
>
> Clement of Alexandria[9]

Sixth century:

> . . . certain men, seized by diabolical incitement, practise among themselves the most disgraceful lusts, and act contrary to nature . . .
>
> Justinian law[10]

Eleventh century:

> To act against nature is always unlawful and beyond doubt more flagrant and shameful than to sin by a natural use in fornication or adultery.
>
> Ivo, Bishop of Chartres[11]

Thirteenth century:

> Just as I ask men whether they committed acts against nature, so I ask women about every type of fornication.
>
> Robert of Flamborough[12]

Seventeenth century:

> Buggery is a detestable and abominable sin, amongst Christians not to be named, committed by carnal knowledge against the ordinance of the Creator, and order of nature.
>
> Edward Coke[13]

Eighteenth century:

> These women . . . are not at all strangers to being willing to seek unnatural pleasures with persons of their own sex.
>
> Moreau de St Mary[14]

Nineteenth century:

> The most melancholy of abasements is that of a hoary and lecherous old man. Filth and obscenity are never so unnaturally nauseous as from the chattering lips of age . . .
>
> *Saturday Review*[15]

Twentieth century:

> The poor homosexuals – they have declared war upon nature, and now nature is exacting an awful retribution.
>
> Patrick J. Buchanan[16]

From time immemorial, it seems, a steady law has held fast: *in the sexual sphere, the good equals the natural*. Does the sheer persistence of this law point beyond the historical enquiry? Does it represent a universal truth, an 'essence'?

Not quite: for the term 'nature' has its own history. This history richly informs the 'nature' which heterosexuality today lays claim to, and it therefore demands to be understood.

5   The History of 'Nature'

In our own time, the word has two broad senses: the total contents of the universe, as in 'the laws of nature'; and the inherent quality of a thing, as in 'the nature of . . . '

It's a strange coupling: everything that is, and the inherent quality of a thing. Not so strange, perhaps, to the first Western philosophers,[17] who sought in *physis* (Greek 'nature') the inherent quality of everything that is. Could it be water? Could it be fire? Could it be air? . . . This ontological ambition was displaced in time by the more modest programme of scientific observation. After Aristotle, the totality of *physis* became the totality of the phenomenal world. It nevertheless remained haunted by the *metaphysis* which it originally embraced, as is evidenced by the ambiguous connotations of our own word 'nature' – connotations at once panoramic and deeply interior.

There is a further sense of 'nature', captured in the expression 'the love of nature'. Here the word is green, a stain whose origins are equally traceable to the early Greeks, and which persisted throughout the long but static episode of scientific endeavour dominated by the relics of Aristotelian thought. In the *Metaphysics*, Aristotle's six-part definition of '*physis*' begins:

> The generation of growing objects.[18]

Nature to the Greek, Roman and Medieval mind was fundamentally organic. While for us, matter is first of all mineral, and only by some mysterious secondary effect gives birth to the swarm of life, for our ancestors, rocks and stones were the slothful organs of an animal planet.

Animals are characterised by movement. But more importantly, they move with purpose. The dog runs to its bone, the bird flies to its nest. And by extension, as Aristotle would have it, the stone falls to the ground.[19] In the animate world, a world of nisus, each entity fulfils a purpose which is intrinsic to its nature.

That this inherent movement may be contradicted by the behaviour of the object – either through external obstruction, or the object's own perversity – yields the possibility of what is designated 'unnatural'. Thus it is that a word which today carries a primarily ethical force has its roots in a certain way of observing the material world.

6 Teleology: Explanation by Purpose

So far as sex is concerned, the crucial legacy of Greek thinking is the identification of nature with purpose. However, this involves us in an ambiguity. Modern science, and hence in a sense modern conscious-ness, founded itself on the rejection of explanation by purpose. We have learnt to ask, 'What made this happen?' rather than, 'To what end does this happen?'

> . . . experience has shown that the mechanistic question leads to scientific knowledge, while the teleological question does not.[20]

The mechanistic question has been posited with a violence which is notorious enough. Mechanical philosophy, which came of age in the seventeenth century and continues to inhabit our own, stills the movement at the heart of things. Before, the cosmos breathed; now it ticks. Stones no longer fly, they're pushed – if nothing pushes them they just sit there: principle of inertia. The planets are lawful but aimless, spinning vacantly round their ellipses in obedience to a forgotten command.[21]

The linguistic effects of this upheaval are clear enough. 'Anima', soul, is replaced by 'vis', force. Robert Boyle, the founder of modern chemistry, proposes banishing the word 'nature' from science altogether.[22] And by an atavistic irony, the old Greek word acquires a new resonance: 'physics'.

In that case, how has 'nature' as we use it today retained its earlier teleology? The answer lies in that field of knowledge whose authority is incessantly invoked by conservative sexual propaganda – biology. Biology is the Achilles heel of the scientific revolution, and the living shrine of an archaic concept of 'nature'. This is not to minimise the genius of Darwin. But it is Darwin's failure, not his achievement, that's at issue here.

Throughout the seventeenth and eighteenth centuries, biology clung to explanation by purpose – the divine purpose of the Creator reflected in the 'fitness for purpose' of each living thing.[23] Darwin's ambition was to dispel this anachronism and qualify his science for membership of a Newtonian universe where the only cause is a past cause. The theory of natural selection explains the illusion of purpose in terms of an arbitrary collision: the struggle for life, individual variants, and environmental changes. Giraffes may *appear* to possess long necks in order to reach their food; in reality, all the short-necked ones died out.

But *The Origin of Species* discloses a subliminal anxiety, something troubling its sturdy fabric. At first, it seems peripheral – a turn of phrase here, an image there. Gradually one realises that the whole text is rotten with the language of intention. The problem is encapsulated in the very expression 'natural *selection*', amplified by 'the struggle *for* life', and sealed by the phenomenon which provided Darwin with his initial stimulus: the human artifice of selective breeding.

Of course, when Darwin writes:

> Man selects only for his own good; Nature only for that of the being which she tends[24]

we understand that it is merely a manner of speaking. Challenged, he would quickly disown a 'tending' Nature.[25] Nevertheless, the accumulated impact of this contrary resonance raises the question of how far one can rescue a logic from the metaphors through which it speaks. In the language of Jacques Derrida, Darwin's structure trembles with the very force it has endeavoured to expunge.[26] And few modern biologists bother to avoid the vocabulary of use, gain and goal which they have neither the means nor the desire to defend. The fact is, if a new enzyme is discovered in the brain of a cat, biological science addresses one over-riding question: what is it *for*?

The history of 'nature' is marked by a certain intransigence: there is something in the concept that has held fast even against the massive transformation of consciousness heralded by Bacon, Descartes, Boyle and Newton. It is this feature – the ineradicable teleology of biological thinking – which makes 'nature' susceptible to capture by an ethical discourse.

If Darwin had succeeded, if modern biology were as rigorously mechanistic as it claims to be, there could be no argument between a natural and a social portrait of the world. In fact, of course, such argument is characteristic of numerous debates – economic, racial and sexual. The contest requires some form of common ground, and this is provided by teleology.

It is impossible to describe either organic or social reality without referring, sooner or later, to the ends to which things move. The biological and the human spheres are both of them dense with aims.

7   *History vs Nature*

The 'nature' of heterosexuality is none other than the 'nature' which has governed the long history of the sexual norm: a 'nature' characterised, even today, by purpose. And this anachronistic teleology in the present sense of 'nature' makes possible a running battle between social and biological justifications – the routine pattern of contemporary dispute.

The agendas are familiar enough. Is the benefit of competition species survival, or class advantage? Are men aggressive in the service of an adaptive or a political end? And heterosexuality – is it the benign implement of a tending nature, or the blunt instrument of masculine tyranny?

The convention among progressive thinkers is to side with the social against the natural. The classic case, perhaps the initial impetus, is Marx's struggle with the conservative economists, his demonstration that capitalism is a man-made structure, not the natural condition of economic life.[27] Indeed, Marx is perceived as having virtually erased 'nature' from the agenda of social analysis:

> Marx rejected the problematic of the earlier philosophy . . . a problematic of human nature.[28]

This is precisely the spirit in which the battles of sexual ideology are currently fought out:

> To be a normal man is to be heterosexual . . . to be a normal woman is to be a welcoming recipient of male wooing . . . But these sharp demarcations are, I would suggest, *historical*, not natural phenomena.[29]

Historical, not natural. Again and again, that is the cry. Simone de Beauvoir paraphrases Merleau-Ponty:

> Man is not a natural species; he is a historical idea.[30]

And Michel Foucault pronounces:

> Sexuality must not be thought of as a kind of natural given which power tries to hold in check, or as an obscure domain which knowledge tries to uncover. It is the name that can be given to a historical construct.[31]

The antithesis of history and nature recurs so frequently, it seems to have acquired an almost unconscious, ritual function.

History currently rules the terms of the sexual debate. But 'nature' is the point at issue. In this situation, the antithesis of history and nature can no longer be taken as read. On the contrary, it must be unravelled before any sense can be made of the 'nature' of heterosexuality.

The problem discussed and the method of discussion are mutually implicated.

8 History Preferred

The privilege accorded to history arises from a certain assumption about what history contributes. According to this outlook, the pursuit of history is a pursuit of origins; in their discovery lies a message of hope – things have not always been this way, therefore they may be changed. By contrast, nature represents the immutable. Thus, an oppression is perceived wherever human law, which is susceptible to revolt, masquerades as natural law, against which there is no appeal. History in this logic is the field of possibility, nature the avatar of a subjugating necessity.

Gay thinkers today are among the most eager participants in this epic combat, and there is no doubt as to where the gay colours are to be pinned. 'Historical' becomes almost synonymous with 'radical', while 'nature' encapsulates everything to be rebutted, deconstructed, restricted and diminished. The chauvinism is usually tempered, of course. Only a fool would deny that nature has a place; but the point is, to keep it there.

The price of this strategy is a price of understanding. The languid detachment that follows from reducing 'essentialist' presumptions to their social antecedents conceals within itself a kind of obtuseness; the quality of vision arrived at possesses a sharpness which is strangely flat. Consider the complaint that rings through most of the past nineteen centuries against the practice of homosexual intercourse: 'It's unnatural!' Historical analysis will certainly illuminate the logic of that virulent cry. But can it grasp the virulence? We may prove that what appeared inscribed by nature was actually scribbled by a human hand. But have we yet registered the hysteria, the violence, above all the *fascination* with which that ageless expression 'contra naturam' is invested?

The evidence from our gay historians isn't good.

This may seem unfair to John Boswell, whose *Christianity, Social Tolerance and Homosexuality* provides a detailed and highly informed discussion of the term 'nature'. However, beyond the historical inquiry, Boswell reveals a surprising lack of curiosity about the concept itself. On the contrary, he is dismissive:

> The objection that homosexuality is 'unnatural' . . . probably represents nothing more than a derogatory epithet of unusual emotional impact due to a confluence of historically sanctioned prejudices and ill-informed ideas . . . [32]

Alan Bray, in his excellent *Homosexuality in Renaissance England*,[33] ascribes the widespread horror of the 'unnatural' he uncovers to a single cause: fear of natural and social catastrophe. The association is well evidenced. Images of plague, deluge and strife certainly attached themselves to the concept of 'sodomite' and a chain of connections was created between sexual order, social order and environmental order. But as Alan Bray himself notes, there was more rant in all this than action. Luridly written laws against 'unnatural' practices were rarely enforced. This discrepancy between texts and actions should alert us to the presence of a submerged significance. If buggery had *literally* been held responsible for bad harvests, we would expect a vigorous pursuit of real culprits by the farmers – not ghoulish sermons from the clerics.

Jeffrey Weeks, in a recent work,[34] documents in vivid and comprehensive detail the recurrence of natural theories in both progressive and reactionary ideologies. But his concern thereafter, like Boswell's, is more to challenge than to elucidate the application of 'nature' to sexual discourse.

A chronicle is not an explanation, and neither is a protest. The mixture of chronicle and protest which characterises the treatment of 'nature' in the work of these three authors leaves the concept unaccountable.

9   The Edge of History

The historical analysis of sexual identities has failed to surmount the problem at issue. But this is not surprising. If heterosexuality raises the question of 'nature' then it simultaneously challenges the competence of history to produce a credible answer. For 'nature' is history's other – as the historians are the first to tell us. 'Historical, not natural' runs the refrain.

The problems I am concerned with are those that appear when this refrain peters out. Why does the appeal to 'nature' so permeate the sexual field? What is the secret of that brutal nausea evoked, even today, by the term 'unnatural'? What is the force of 'nature' in the promulgation of erotic virtue? The *force*, let me stress, not the genealogy.

My answer would be: the very rupture which separates history from nature. This is the wound that normative sexuality seeks to heal. But from where should it be perceived? From within history, or from within 'nature'? The objection to the former is that historicism, by claiming a total perspective, denies the rupture; 'nature' commonly appears to the historian as subordinate territory, a formless mass waiting to be stamped with social meanings.

Suppose then, we approach the problem from the other side of the divide, from within 'nature'?

10   The Edge of Nature

In a quite different way, 'nature' also lays claim to totality:

> All phenomena exist in one nature, and must so exist, inasmuch as without this *a priori* unity, no unity of experience, and consequently no determination of objects in experience, is possible.[35]

But it's a striking fact that while 'nature' means everything there is – the existence of all phenomena – it nevertheless admits of exceptions. For example, Aristotle observes that money 'exists not by nature but by law'. And Seneca advises: 'nature does not bestow virtue – it is an art to be good'.[37] Art (in the sense of the Greek term *techne*) and law (in the sense of social convention) are classically excluded from the totality which is *physis*. This inconsistency is not the consequence of some minor frivolity in the development of the language; it is rather a betrayal by the language of an unhappy wisdom.

Although nature is all phenomena, neither art nor law are regarded as 'natural'. But why? What strange property drives them out of the completed universe of which they nevertheless remain a part?

The answer is simple enough: humanity. Nothing is 'unnatural' which is not human.

And this is precisely the sense of the familiar antithesis of 'history' and 'nature'. 'History' in this opposition has none other than a human meaning. Faced with 'nature', in fact, 'history' and 'human' appear irreducibly synonymous.

But we run aground at once. The antithesis of the human and the natural is no sooner established than it is compromised by a naked and obtrusive presence – the human body. Nothing is unnatural which is not human, but not everything human is unnatural. The position is absolutely ambiguous.

The ambiguity may be characterised as a rift – actually, a double rift.

Nature in its totality is split by human being; human being in its singularity is split by nature.

Can a statement of such large simplicity be pronounced without a flutter of embarrassment? Neither 'human' nor 'being' are comfortably spoken in the polite society of postmodernist discourse.[38] Contemporary intellectual manners require a kind of salon irony, in which words rarely rise above their character as text.

Too bad. The appeal to nature inherent in heterosexual supremacism provokes a question whose terms are bluntly ontological: a question of being. The problem of the natural and the human is a problem of the nature *of* the human. Such is the consequence of moving towards the limit of 'history' on the one hand, and towards the limit of 'nature' on the other.

The conceptual difficulties here are considerable – perhaps insurmountable. But that is because the *actual* difficulties, suffered within our lived experience, are themselves considerable. And perhaps insurmountable. It's these living difficulties which give rise to the monstrous and seductive claims of 'natural' sexuality.

11   The Human and the Natural – 1

Clearly, the 'nature' of heterosexuality will not disclose itself to a purely historical gaze. After all, the problem touched by 'nature' is inherently transhistorical – that is, transhuman. Nevertheless, the problem is encountered exclusively *within* human experience – that is, within history. It is only in the historical narrative that the ontological question acquires a form – or rather, a multiplicity of forms – by which it can make itself known to us.

The task now is to investigate these forms, using history to uncover them, but not submitting to history in the effort to understand them.

Of the myriad ways by which humanity has distinguished itself from nature, there are a few key concepts which bear directly on the field of sexuality. Whether optimistic or pessimistic, these distinctions are concerned with how humanity is grounded in the totality of which it is but one component. The issue at all points is our being-in-the-world: the strength or fragility of the hyphens.

Optimistically, we have inherited from Greece the distinction of reason, and from Israel the distinction of dominion.

As regards reason, it appears in the first place as the quintessential anomaly of human being, the gift which sets us apart from the world and from that within us which is *of* the world: thus, we are 'rational animals'. But because the Greeks came to identify reason with the real – to regard the essence of the world as Idea rather than matter – this same peculiarity recombines us with the whole from which it seems to mark us off. Reason – and philosophy in particular – enables humanity to penetrate the illusory alienation of *physis* and embrace the underlying unity which is *metaphysis*.

As for the Hebraic legacy, there is, of course, no synonym for *physis* in either the Old Testament or the Gospels. The nearest equivalent – near enough to be integrated with it in a later age – is the 'created world'. The spectacular assembly of sky, mountains, oceans, animals and plants is a key protagonist in the Biblical texts, from Genesis to the Book of Revelation. Standing outside it, but informing every detail, God the creator establishes for humanity a position within the spectacle which is both unique and harmonious. Humanity is distinguished from creation not, this time, by virtue of reason, but through *dominion* – lordship over our own habitation.[39] As reason permits Greek humanity to participate in the transcendent Idea, so dominion permits Hebrew humanity to participate in the transcendent power of God.

Conjoined as they become in the elaborate and quarrelsome literature of Medieval theology, these two – dominion and reason – do not properly coalesce until the Renaissance gives birth to modern science. For it is in consequence of this moment that reason begins to govern technological practice. Now 'mind' in the Greek sense – a sense shaped by mathematics – acquires a new and awesome separateness:

> Reason is just as cunning as she is powerful . . . causing objects to act and react on each other in accordance with their own nature.[40]

With this perception, Hegel paves the way for Marx to establish production as the peculiar mark of human being:

> Men can be distinguished from animals by consciousness, by religion, or anything else you like. They themselves begin to distinguish themselves from animals as soon as they *produce* their means of subsistence.[41]

It is, of course, *reasoned* production, for Marx acknowledges, a little belatedly, that many other creatures produce the means of their subsistence:

> . . . what distinguishes the worst architect from the best of bees is this, that the architect raises his structure in his imagination before he erects it in reality.[42]

Here, we reach a point in which humanity's relation to natural reality is characterised by *rational dominion*. It is on this basis that Marx can promise, as the *telos* of the communist enterprise, that state of perfect integration in which 'human history becomes natural history, and natural history becomes human history'.[43]

12 The Human and the Natural – 2

These themes simultaneously project the shadows of a pessimistic vision – an intimation that there is a split inherent in the human condition, separating us from the world we inhabit, and from our own actuality. The Hebraic tradition confers on it an ethical vocabulary. Sin, to the Christian mind and its prophetic forerunners is not incidental, but structural: to be born is to lapse. And through the myths which articulate it, the idea of sin is thoroughly implicated in the idea of nature.

The narrative of Eden portrays, as the point from which we have already fallen, a garden of ontological wholeness. Originally, Adam is a friend of the animals, naked as they are. He is a being of the same order, at home with them in a shared environment, distinguished only by the privilege of his stewardship. The moment of sin is the moment of exile: a breach in his being-in-the-world.

Adam's departure from Eden is *Adam*'s fault, not God's. This is critical: for if God were to blame, what hope for restoration could we ever harbour? A dreadful burden of guilt protects the dream of future deliverance. One day God will come to heal humanity's fractured circumstance, but in the meantime, we are to blame for our own alienation. Guilt is the price of the Messianic promise.

Following Adam's explusion, 'humanity' becomes the mark of foreignness. A moat now separates the human island from the rest of the world. Adam wears clothes: culture is born, simultaneously shutting out external nature and concealing nature within. But Adam's 'nature within' struggles to burst out, like a bird trapped in a building. It strives to rejoin, as it were, the nature without from which it has been divorced. Such is the urgency of the flesh: the frantic beating of wings, the efforts of a being in search of its own completion.

But this complaint of the flesh against its imprisonment in culture is a reminder of an alienation humanity prefers to forget. And a reminder, too, of the intolerable guilt for it which we have assumed. The nisus of the flesh is therefore identified with the burden of sin, and we turn on both with loathing.

The Greek privilege of reason, no less than the Hebraic status of dominion, has been scarred by a tragic apprehension. This becomes apparent from the moment reason reaches, in the modern age, its apotheosis.

The displacement of *physis*, in its organic and purposive vitality, by the inert universe of mechanical philosophy, gives birth to that inconsolable division of mind and matter which is our Cartesian inheritance. Human consciousness surveys the machine-world and the machine-body which it now inhabits, and finds itself a stranger. 'Nature' in its earlier character is exiled henceforth to the dangerous wilderness of Romantic nostalgia, the necessary antidote to scientific triumphalism.

In two radically different traditions, and in the modern consciousness they have parented, the human and the natural appear to be at odds. If the singularity of our species may be experienced as a kind of jubilation, it is no less often suffered as an injury. The ontological problem is one of discontinuity: a break in the line that runs from the centre of human subjectivity to the ground on which we stand.

In so far as we find ourselves different from our world, this difference does not lie solely outside, at the point where the city of artefacts yields to its organic environment. We carry it within. That we have ceased to search, in the manner of Descartes, for a tangible border-post, a pineal gland, is simply a measure of our increased despair. The problem is the body.

13 Sex

The body is the epicentre of an ontological dilemma which has been variously articulated, but which can be securely phrased in terms of 'nature'. My body, in its chemistry, its structure, its reflexes and its hungers is incontestably continuous with the natural world. But – how far am I continuous with my body, and therefore with my total context?

'Sex' arises here as a way to characterise the body, and hence the embodied subject, not only in its substance, but in its situation. To account for the body in sexual terms is to *position it in the world* in a certain way. And the position is quite different from that implied by an economic account, or an instrumental account, or a mechanistic account. The language of sex fashions a unique relation of the interior to the exterior. In so far as heterosexuality lays claim to the heart of sexual reality, to be what sex properly is, it presumes at the same time to dictate the form of this relation.

The question is: how has sex been used to articulate our being-in-the-world?

Over the last hundred years or so, the volume of sexual discourse has inexorably swollen. This mass of sex-talk, witheringly charted by Michel Foucault and his followers, has acquired a complexity which defies any single interpretation. Nevertheless, there are two important points whose obviousness seems to have deprived them of a central position in the new sexual histories. They are both points of context.

In the West, the past century has been characterised by a collapse in religious belief, and by a drastic spread of urbanisation. These twin developments, silently accompanying the flood of sexual chatter, bear directly on the issue I am trying to hold in view: the place of the human species in the totality which sustains it.

The industrial revolution inflicted a violent dislocation, wrenching humanity from a proximate, if uneasy, relation to its natural environment. And with the passing of religious consensus – albeit only a consensus of terms – there is no universal language through which to redefine our position. In this situation, sex has assumed a mystic, and mystifying, importance.

14   Sex and Religion

When Foucault says that sex has come to represent 'the truth of our being',[44] he chooses an ontological turn of phrase – no less so for being spoken, in the contemporary manner, with a bemused sigh. For two millenia the 'truth of our being' was the almost exclusive preserve of the Christian religion.

It is only during the nineteenth and twentieth centuries that Christianity ceased to provide the West with its dominant ontology – the broad terms in which people account for their existence. At the same time, sexual discourse, hitherto subordinated for the most part to Christian ideology, began its astonishing expansion. Passing out of ecclesiastical control through the medical and psychoanalytic institutions, it eventually took up residence in the garish constellation of media and mass production which the Situationists have called 'the commodity spectacle'.[45] Today, it is easier to escape the voice of God than to hold oneself aloof from the daily barrage of sexual imagery and exhortation.

The profane trespass of sexuality was recognised early on. Freud's atheism was no mere fad: at some level, he recognised that what he was conferring on Eros had been stolen from a younger deity. Not, of course, that Freud was foolish enough to worship sex (as Reich came to); but he made of it an axis of self-definition that would never tolerate the rivalry of a theist *weltanschauung*. In this, he was both a contributor to and exemplar of that garrulous torrent which Foucault has described and denounced. Sex today is not a religion – that would be a facile equation – but it has flooded into many of the spaces which religion has vacated.

15   Sex and the City

In *Sexuality and its Discontents*, Jeffrey Weeks follows Foucault in criticising the opposition – which reaches its apotheosis in Reich – between sex as a raw instinctual force on the one hand, and the constraints of civilisation on the other. The essence of the criticism is that what we know as 'sex' has no existence independent of the cultural values which define it, order it, and present it to consciousness. The biological reality is contaminated through and through with social meanings.

In a sense, this critique is irrefutable. We cannot step outside our historical – that is, our human – condition and serenely compare, as if from an equidistant platform, the thing we are with the thing we are not. But this is the crucial point: a point of pain before it is a point of intellectual dispute. Consciousness is a finitude we have to acknowledge, but can never surpass. The boundary of human culture is unknowable – we know this today perhaps better than ever before. But we do not know that there is no boundary. On the contrary, there must be one. And what was formerly understood – for example in the naive opposition of instinct and civilisation – is that every intimation of this boundary is potentially a trauma.

Merely deconstructing sex fails to articulate the anxiety that the construct represents.

The traumatic inaccessibility of a nature which is both beyond and within us has received its most potent – and anxious – expression in the Romantic protest. The unkempt landscapes of Wordsworth's poetry, Melville's fiction, Wagner's theatre, or Turner's canvasses contrast eloquently with the genially tended meadows which pleased a pre-industrial imagination. In the presence of 'dark satanic mills', a new, defensive value attaches itself to nature in the rough.

Sex, in the contemporaneous tide of sexual discourse, takes sides with Romanticism in the same struggle. Sex is our allotment – in the heart of the city, our little square of heath. To make love, we fling off our clothes, abandoning the signs which mark us as civilised: law, art and language. This is what makes sex startling, like hair growing on a telephone. And precious – the very last of our savings from a lost affluence. Sex, then, has been appointed as the domain – finite, controllable, nameable – within which we can experience ourselves as at once natural and human: that is, as beings continuous with the world beyond culture's indiscernible edge.

16   Why Sex?

The decline of religion and the rise of the industrial city have given a new poignancy to the ontological status accorded to sexuality. But they do not account for it. As I have already indicated, the formula 'good sex is natural sex' is as old as Christianity; and it can be tracked into the deeper past of Stoic philosophy.

Furthermore, even the sexual dissidents have colluded with the ancient rule. Earlier this century, homosexual propagandists such as Magnus Hirschfield and André Gide[46] argued that their proclivities were 'natural' after all. Today it is felt more decorous to discount nature altogether. Nobody – except perhaps the self-conscious decadent[47] – wants to be caught embracing an 'unnatural' sexuality. If nature has any say, even among the rebels, then nature dictates the good.

This implicit consensus masks its *arbitrary* character. The unasked question is: why is the good identified with the natural in relation to *sex*? Why not in respect of transport, or music, or truth?

A heterosexual friend to whom I mentioned that I was writing this essay supplemented his words of encouragement with a warning: 'It's all very well, you know, but you can't argue with biology.' Has he never fried an egg? The whole of human history is an 'argument with biology'. The very civilisation which the most homophobic ideologues are eager to defend is the *antithesis* of nature: law and art.

This logical oddity is most transparent when appeals are made – as they have been recurrently since Aquinas and before – to the animal kingdom. The animals serve simultaneously as the model of sexual decorum, and the very type of debasement. Thus (in truly Thomist vein) the self-annointed 'defender' of heterosexuality:

> Human sexuality is a continuum of nature – animal, human, and self. Unless we understand this, we are in danger of becoming lower animals only.[48]

Herein lies the mystery of the sexual prohibitions. The crime of sodomy represents at once a descent to the pigsty, and the failure to behave like a proper pig.

The point is this: that the natural ethic, taken to its logical conclusion, would cancel humanity altogether. Hence it is confined, in a transparently irrational fashion, to the sexual field. Human *sexuality* is proclaimed a 'continuum of nature' – not human government, or human poetry, or human aviation, or human gateau. AIDS is 'nature's retribution'; a collapsing tower block isn't. Where it is promulgated, the law of nature is absolute, and carries the power of life or death. But it is only promulgated in one or two territories: pre-eminently, sex. The assumption on which the heterosexual imperative founds itself is radically inconsistent.[49]

But still the question is: why sex? What is it about sexuality that selects it as almost *uniquely* the field of the 'natural' and so conceals this selection as to make it appear self-evident? How is the nature of sex turned into the sovereignty of nature?

17   Sex as Procreation

Classically speaking, the nature of a thing, its inner truth, is given by its purpose; that is to say, the proper end of its movement. When sexuality is challenged in these terms, the response appears self-evident. The purpose of sex is procreation.

Yet this self-evident answer begs the question. It is the answer which arises from already positioning human sexuality in the wider *physis* – among the plants and animals of external nature – as opposed to locating it in the field of human history, that is, the history of *human* purposes.

It is true that the procreative function has conventionally decided between 'natural' and 'unnatural' sexual practice, and today lends its authority to heterosexual supremacy. But sex has always offered itself for other uses – recreation, domination, profit, romance . . . Repositioned among the laws and artefacts of culture, sex is no more self-evidently *for* procreation than the mouth is for eating, rather than singing hymns.

We see here that the priority given to procreation *follows* from the use of sexuality as a bridge between the inner and the outer *physis*.

Procreation alone does not explain why sex is selected as the field of the natural. This is confirmed by contemporary experience: millions of people use contraceptives without compunction (*pace* the Vatican) but retain their disgust at the 'unnaturalness' of homosexual activity. What they find 'natural' in their heterosexuality is not, or not only, the production of babies.

18   Woman and Man

In the Medieval diatribes, the distinction between natural and unnatural sex pivoted on what Freud has called the 'aim': hand, anus, mouth, thigh, etc. Today, we are more concerned with the 'object': do what you like, but do it with the right person. This historical change is one of degree, and can be exaggerated. If the gender connotations of 'heterosexuality' have moved into the foreground, it is because of disturbances in the gender structure provoked by the feminist and gay movements. What is now asserted was before assumed. Unchanged is the criterion of 'nature'.

Of interest here is the archaic identification of woman with nature – Simone de Beauvoir's preoccupation. The function thereby imposed on woman is to soften the distinction between the human and the natural. This is why the texts which enshrine her oppression are always couched in terms of degree. Woman is not '*irrational*' – she is '*less*' rational'. Conversely, she is not 'tender', 'intuitive' and 'sensuous' to the exclusion of man. She is just 'more' all these things than he. It is the simultaneous sameness and difference of woman that promises to carry man back towards nature without destroying his human privilege.

Like procreation, the images of gender contribute to the ontological function assigned to sexuality. But they, too, fail to complete the picture.

19   Desire

We cannot be done with this question of sex without re-entering that interior from which we are always liable to be driven by the admonishments of social history. Sex is also lust. To characterise sex as 'the truth of our being' is to identify our being with our desires. Now the subjective character of desire – even in its most solitary moments – is self-transcendent. Desire is desire *for*. It leans out of its own window. It hails what is beyond itself.

Retrospectively, the neurologist, the behaviourist or the historian may construct past causes for my sexual acts. But in the moment of lust, I am all future. Sexual longing is as teleological in character as the flora and fauna of Galapagos. Like the organic life-force that disrupted Darwin's scientific enterprise, lust struggles towards what has yet to be. Thus it is more than a merely formal recognition that invites us to set Eros on the side of *physis*, against the machine.[50] What is the folk image of human sex? – the birds and the bees, precisely!

Indeed, of all our material needs, sex is singular in its imperviousness to technical transformation, and hence to the history which technology gives rise to. As Marx observed, 'the hunger which is gratified by cooked meat eaten with a knife and fork is a different hunger from that which bolts down raw meat with the aid of hand, nail and tooth.'[51] Stubbornly palaeolithic, sex is as raw today as it ever was. You can't cook fellatio. Be it 2,000 BC or 2,000 AD, you just suck.

20   Nature in Crisis

So what is the truth of the matter? Is sex *in fact* the privileged avenue from culture to nature? Or is it merely a sign that has been erected in the hope – or the despair – of completing that ineffable journey?

No hesitation here: the sexual norm represents a fatuous attempt to square the circle described by 'nature'. And the fatuity has grown in proportion with the recent aggrandisement of sexual discourse.

The ontological quest which sex has been commanded to serve is for a reconciliation of the human and the natural; and this 'natural' embraces a double sense, both the body and the world it inhabits. In respect of the latter, however, a whole new problem has arisen – one that lies far beyond the grasp of any conceivable sexual terminology. In the course of the past few decades, the external basis of human existence has been thrown into peril.

The threat of ecological catastrophe that distinguishes this century lies outside the scope of my discussion, but is nevertheless its proper context. The suicidal ravages now being inflicted on external *physis*, our living habitation, lend an entirely new dimension to the significance of 'nature'.

The crisis requires that a new subtlety be brought to the uses made of this term, an attitude of care and questioning which surpasses the routine antinomies of current debates.

To perpetuate a vulgar chauvinism – 'history, not nature' – in the name of sexual liberation is to risk disarmament in the struggle to redeem the environment. And while the surrender to 'nature' proposed by the sexual norm is untenable, the *disparagement* of 'nature' cultivated by radical historicism may collude with history's destruction. The birds and the bees of heterosexual mythology are risible; but in many parts of the globe, *real* birds and bees are threatened with extinction.

In that case, might not a return to 'natural' sexuality herald the beginning of a healthier accommodation to the biosphere? Could heterosexuality be relaunched as a kind of erotic vegetarianism?

To argue this would be to misunderstand the spirit of the sexual norm, which is fundamentally whimsical. It bears an antithetical, not an exemplary relation to the civilised world: in bed we are the more animal, so that out of it we may be the less so. The ethic of sexual normality – the good is the natural – is untransferrable to human culture precisley because, in its absoluteness, it denies the possibility of culture. 'Heterosexuality', as the norm is now called, has the conservative function of a fiesta: a ritual regression to untransformed nature which distracts us from the poison of our constructed environment. It is the official nature reserve that sanctions the surrounding devastation. As such it does not spread its natural values, but hoards them jealously. The myth of 'natural love' is purely gestural, like a potted plant in an asbestos factory.

There is urgent need of a new contract with the natural world from which we draw breath. The 'heterosexual' ideal cannot model this contract. On the contrary, it stands in the way, because it refuses to admit the necessary sense in which to be human is *not* to be continuous with nature. This truth, sad and hard, ought to be grasped once and for all, without nostalgia and without violence.

There is not, and never was, an Eden. No singularity of being-in-the-world is available: neither through primitive regression nor through technological mastery. The totality of nature and the totality of history are spectral empires engaged in a spectral battle. The reality is partial, torn, indefinite and unpossessable: we are out of place, strangers in our own home. This is the context in which the sexual crisis, and equally the ecological crisis, needs to be confronted. So far as I can see, the only credible objective, modest and incomplete, is an endless, gradually improving negotiation between the human and the natural – within and without us.

21   Ends

What is the appropriate language of this negotiation? The science of biology, in its failure to accommodate the mechanical universe, suggests the terms in which the human and the non-human can converse. *Physis* is a world of ends. The 'natural given' is not a given object, nor a given force, but a given *purpose*. I do not mean, of course, the monolithic purpose of a divine plan, but the myriad, highly specific purposes that interlock to compose the biosphere. Each species, as Aristotle observed, contains its end within itself.

At the same time, purpose is the raw material of human action, of human politics.

There are purposes we create, and purposes we discover within and

around us. We cannot *identify* our purposes with those of the animals
and the plants: that's the reactionary sentimentality of 'natural' sex.
Nor is there any hope left in the mastery of nature – a wholesale
subjugation of all natural purposes to our own such as underwrites the
Marxist promise. The need is rather to inhabit, and observe, a
multiplicity of ends whose inter-relations shift constantly, in response
to natural accident and our own interventions.

To my understanding, no fixed rules can govern our participation in
this matrix: not in the sexual sphere, nor in any other. In our
negotiation between natural and human objectives, we simply have to
see what works.

For example: consider the purpose of the penis. Biologically
speaking, it's quite obvious that the relation of the penis to the vagina is
not equivalent to the relation of the penis to the anus. Apart from its
urinary function, the penis is *for* inserting into the vagina to deliver
semen.[52] That is its 'nature', its given purpose. But without harm, I've
invested mine with a different purpose – pleasure and love.

22   *Heterosexuality Revisited*

But why should such an investment be at all restricted? Isn't an
equivalent shift of purpose possible in a heterosexual coupling? Could
heterosexuality not be rescued from the *ancien régime* of 'nature'?

One imagines here a re-presentation of male–female intercourse as a
freely chosen option, claiming no privilege among erotic games because
its relation to biological function has been transformed from one of
determination to one of *coincidence*. I believe this is the only tenable
future for heterosexuality. But liberty is indivisible in the sexual sphere
as everywhere else. So long as lesbians and gay men suffer the assaults
of its 'natural' pretensions, heterosexuality will remain a prison – even
for the nicest warders. Freedom for heterosexuals will only be found
where those whom they have oppressed are already seeking it: on that
uneasy margin of the natural world which is called the human
condition.[53]

Notes

1. I suppose it is traceable to Marx. See the *Theses on Feuerbach*: 'Feuerbach resolves the essence of religion into the essence of *man*. But the essence of man is no abstraction inherent in each single individual. In its reality it is the ensemble of the social relations.' For a vigorous and relevant reiteration see Jeffrey Weeks, *Sex, Politics and Society*, especially the first chapter.
2. For the 'social construction' of homosexuality, see Kenneth Plumber (ed.), *The Making of the Modern Homosexual*, London 1981.
3. Jonathan Katz, 'The invention of heterosexuality, 1892–1982' in Supplement II, papers of the conference 'Among Men, Among Women', University of Amsterdam, 1983. (The summary history which follows this reference is my own version of events, not a précis of that work.)
4. See, for example, Havelock Ellis, *Man and Woman*.
5. Stanley Keleman, *In Defense of Heterosexuality*, Berkeley 1982.
6. See for example, Alan Bray's criticisms of his fellow historian, John Boswell. Alan Bray, *Homosexuality in Renaissance England*, London 1982, p. 8.
7. For a useful survey, see Janet Sayers, *Biological Politics: Feminist and Anti-Feminist Perspectives*, London 1982.
8. Romans 1, 26–27.
9. Quoted from *Paedagogus* 2.10 by John Boswell in *Christianity, Social Tolerance and Homosexuality. Gay People in Western Europe from the Beginning of the Christian Era to the Fourteenth Century*, Chicago and London 1980, p. 147.
10. Quoted from *Novel 77* by D.S. Bailey in *Homosexuality and the Western Christian Tradition*, London 1955, pp. 73–74.
11. Quoted from *Decretum* par. IX, cap 106, by Vern L. Bullough in *Sexual Variance in Society and History*, New York 1976.
12. Thomas Aquinas, *Summa Theologica*, Part I of Second Part, Q. 94, Art. 3., Chicago 1952, p. 223. The point is justified by provisionally defining 'human nature' as 'that nature which is common to man and other animals'.
13. Edward Coke, *The Third Part of the Institutes of the Laws of England: Concerning High Treason, and Other Pleas of the Crown, and Criminal Causes*, London 1644, p. 58.
14. Quoted in Bullough, op. cit.
15. Quoted by Eric Tudgill in *Madonnas and Magdalens: the Origins and Development of Victorian Sexual Attitudes*, London 1976, p. 140.
16. Quoted from *New York Post* (24 May 1983) by Jeffrey Weeks in *Sexuality and its Discontents: Meanings, Myths and Modern Sexualities*, London 1985, p. 48.
17. For a scrupulous discussion of the use made of '*physis*' by the Ionian presocratics, see R. G. Collingwood, *The Idea of Nature*, Oxford 1945.
18. *Aristotle's Metaphysics*, translated by Hippocrates G. Apostle, Bloomington and London 1966, p. 77.

19. 'The stone which by nature falls downwards cannot be habituated to move upwards, not even if one tries to train it by throwing it up ten thousand times.' Aristotle, *Nicomachean Ethics*, translated by D. Ross, Oxford 1954.

20. Bertrand Russell, *A History of Western Philosophy*, London 1984 (first published 1946), pp. 84–85.

21. See Collingwood, op. cit., p. 5.

22. See Robert Boyle, *A Free Enquiry into the Vulgarly Receiv'd Notion of Nature*, London 1685.

23. For an influential example of this tradition, see William Paley, *Natural Theology*, London 1802.

24. Charles Darwin, *The Origin of Species*, Harmondsworth 1968, p. 132.

25. Occasionally, the problem becomes so acute that Darwin explicitly corrects himself. For example, see Darwin, op. cit., p. 16.

26. See the essay on Foucault in Jacques Derrida, *Writing and Difference*, translated by Alan Bass, London and Henley 1978.

27. See the opening passages of *Grundrisse*. A useful selection has been translated by David McLellan: *Marx's Grundrisse*, St Albans 1973.

28. Louis Althusser, *For Marx*, London 1969, pp. 227–228. For a pithy and indignant rebuttal of this assertion, see Norman Geras, *Marx and Human Nature: Refutation of a Legend*, London 1983.

29. Jeffrey Weeks, op. cit., p. 86.

30. Simone de Beauvoir, *The Second Sex* translated by H.M. Parshley, Harmondsworth 1983, p. 66.

31. Michel Foucault, *The History of Sexuality Volume 1: an Introduction*, Harmondsworth 1981.

32. John Boswell, op. cit., Chicago and London 1980.

33. Alan Bray, op. cit.

34. Jeffrey Weeks, op. cit.

35. Immanuel Kant, *Critique of Pure Reason*, London and New York 1934, p. 164.

36. Aristotle, op. cit.

37. Quoted from *Epistles* 90:45 in Boswell, op. cit. p. 150.

38. Throw in 'purpose', 'freedom' and 'commitment' and you have spelt the name of Sartre.

39. 'And God said, let us make man in our image, after our likeness: and let them have dominion over the fish of the sea, and over the fowl of the air, and over the cattle, and over all the earth, and over every creeping thing that creepeth upon the earth.' Genesis 1. 26.

40. Quoted from Hegel's *Logic* in Karl Marx, *Capital* I, 1887, p. 199n.

41. Quoted from *Marx-Engels Gesamtausgabe* in T.B. Bottomore and M. Rubel (eds), *Karl Marx Selected Writings in Sociology and Social Philosophy*, Harmondsworth 1963, p. 69.

42. Karl Marx, *Capital* I, pp. 198–199.

43. Or again: 'Communism as complete naturalism is humanism, and as a complete humanism is naturalism. It is the *definite* resolution of the antagonism between man and Nature . . . ' Quoted from *Marx-Engels Gesamtausgabe* in T.B. Bottomore and M. Rubel, op. cit., p. 250.

44. Michel Foucault, op. cit.

45. See for example, *Leaving the Twentieth Century: the Incomplete Work of the Situationist International*, London 1974.
46. Gide's polemic on this subject has been reissued by GMP: André Gide, *Corydon*, translated by Richard Howard, London 1985. 'Natural' homosexuality is a hoary defence. Here is Arnold Vernoille in 1323: ' . . . if a man plays with another, and because of the warmth of their bodies semen flows, it is not as grave a sin as if a man carnally knows a woman; because . . . nature demands this and a man is made healthier as a result.' Quoted in Michael Goodich, op. cit., p. 95. See also Boswell, op. cit.
47. For example, Jorris Huysmans. Or Wilde in his wilder moments. Also Quentin Crisp, who on television has advised against confusing the good with the natural.
48. Stanley Keleman, op. cit., p. 93. On Thomas Aquinas's muddled appeal to animal conduct, see Boswell, op. cit., p. 318 f.
49. It may be objected that 'nature' is the key saleable value in today's retail markets: natural food, natural furniture, natural shoes, natural toothpaste . . . The Romantic landscape has become a list of ingredients. This unnerving development warrants analysis in terms of ecological anxiety in the first place, and ontological anxiety in the second. But sexuality hasn't yet been robbed of its peculiar distinction, namely that it confers on 'nature' an *ethical* value. To eat white bread is unwise; to be fucked in the arse is immoral. Of course, this may change.
50. I am paddling upstream against Deleuze and Guattari's 'desiring machines' (*Anti-Oedipus: Capitalism and Schizophrenia*). But their use of 'desire' is so remote from ordinary language ('I want') that it's almost out of earshot.
51. From *Grundrisse*. McLellan, op. cit., p. 35.
52. I am not stopping to argue with the idea that homosexuality or bisexuality have some mysterious adaptive function. The biological facts of anatomy are plain for all to see. Freud's 'innate bisexuality', for example, is not a biological discovery – it's a psychologist's ruse.
53. One or two readers of this essay have protested that I have failed to address the question of power. I plead: of current terms, I find 'power' the most problematical, because it is used, even by Foucault, as if it contained its own explanation. The sexual field is saturated with power – I don't deny that. But the question *why power?* continues to be begged. It is too large a question to fit on these few pages. In a sense, though, it is the reason they are written.

Notes on the Contributors

Diana Chapman

Born in Bristol in 1928 with the Sun in Taurus, Moon in Libra and Sagittarius rising. Was the result of a mésalliance between Doris Quant and William Chapman. Being struck with penis envy in the back garden at the age of six, she has spent the greater part of her life resenting being female and envying men. She has accordingly embraced both lesbianism and feminism but recently has begun to wonder whether her claims to either are not rather tenuous. Nevertheless, in view of the appalling state of play between the sexes, she is currently of the opinion that although lesbianism is no great shakes – what else is there?

Kate Charlesworth

is a freelance cartoonist and illustrator whose work appears regularly in *Radio Times*, *New Scientist*, *New Society* and other periodical publications. Her collection *Exotic Species* was published by GMP in 1984. She worked with Marsaili Cameron on *All That*, an illustrated text about women's history which was published by Pandora in 1986.

Joan Crawford

has been a schoolteacher in Africa, a freelance broadcaster in London for the Canadian Broadcasting Corporation, a documentary film researcher, a co-founder and co-artistic director of the King's Head Theatre, Islington (and thereby a lady publican), an industrial psychologist and a director of a literary agency. Throughout this varied career she has successfully resisted the temptation to put pen to paper; this contribution, therefore, represents her first literary endeavour. From her wide experience of writers at work she suspects that, had she any sense, she should stop here.

Pete Freer

is attached to the Centre for Contemporary Cultural Studies at Birmingham University and works at Oval House Arts Centre in London.

Noël Greig

Previous publications with GMP have been the Introduction to the three-volume edition of Edward Carpenter's *Selected Writings*, and three of his plays – *As Time Goes By* (co-written with the late Drew Griffiths), *The Dear Love of Comrades* and *Poppies*. He began writing in the 1960s through his work with various radical theatre companies; organisations he's been involved with include The Combination, Inter-Action, The General Will, Bradford GLF Theatre, Gay Sweatshop and Oval House. Recent plays include *The Death of Christopher Marlowe*, *Spinning a Yarn*, *Best of Friends*, *Do We Ever See Grace* and *Rainbow's Ending*. Noël Greig is a director of Gay Sweatshop Theatre Company.

Robert Glück

lives in San Francisco where he is assistant director of the Poetry Centre at San Francisco State University. His most recent books include *Elements of a Coffee Service*, a book of stories (Four Seasons Foundation), and *La Fontaine*, a book of rewritings in collaboration with Bruce Boone (Black Star Series). *Jack the Modernist*, a novel, is published in Britain by GMP. Enola Gay continues to cause as much trouble as possible, with a double focus these days on AIDS funding and US policy in Central America.

Gillian E. Hanscombe

was born, bred, educated, socialised and psychoanalysed in Australia. She has lived in England since 1969 and has worked variously as a teacher, lecturer, cleaner, typist, insurance saleswoman, mother and writer. She is a partner in the freelance firm Cameron & Hanscombe, which undertakes copywriting, editing, journalism and the construction of distance learning and teaching materials. Her books include *Rocking the Cradle: Lesbian Mothers* (with Jackie Forster); *Between Friends* (a novel); *Title Fight: The Battle for Gay News* (with Andrew Lumsden); *The Art of Life – Dorothy Richardson and the development of feminist consciousness*; a cycle of poems, *Hecate's Charms*; and *Flesh and Paper* (with Suniti Namjoshi, Jezebel Tapes and Books 1987).

Alison Hennegan

was literary editor of the original *Gay News* from 1977 to 1983. Since January 1984 she has been editor of The Women's Press Bookclub. She writes regularly for the *New Statesman* and has contributed articles to *Homosexuality, Power and Politics* (Alison & Busby), *On Gender and Writing* (Pandora) and *Truth, Dare or Promise* (Virago). She has written the introductions for *Girls Next Door: Lesbian Feminist Stories* (The Women's Press), and for reprints of Radclyffe Hall's *The Well of Loneliness* and *Adam's Breed* (both Virago) and Rosemary Manning's *The Chinese Garden* (Brilliance Books).

Rosanna Hibbert

'I am not well educated and have no qualifications. Partly because of this I am now in the middle of my third unbrilliant career, having failed to be heard as a singer and grown out of copywriting. I was born in 1932 and try not to feel passée, but it is difficult now that women are called "older" (a kind word for "old") at 35. In spite of all this I regret very little except my late acceptance of lesbianism and chronic unawareness of feminism and its history.'

Martin Humphries

is a poet and writer. Publications include two books of poetry *Mirrors* (1980), *Searching for a Destination* (1982), and *Not Love Alone: a modern gay anthology* (GMP 1985) which he compiled. Whilst working at Oval House Arts and Community Centre he was a member of the Achilles Heel collective which led directly to the publication of *The Sexuality of Men* (Pluto 1985) co-edited with Andy Metcalf.

Kris Kirk

is prolific though highly neurotic freelance writer, whose work appears in *Gay Times*, *Melody Maker*, *The Face*, *City Limits*, *Smash Hits*, blah, blah. Author of *Men in Frocks* (with photographer Ed Heath, his lover), Kris is presently driving his fellow-householders – three men, four cats, two terrapins and a parrot – totally haywire by completing a book for GMP on gays in pop, *The Vinyl Closet*. *A Boy Called Mary* – a one-hour tv drama-doc about Kris's life – was shown on Channel 4 in November 1986. Like Kim Novak, his favourite colour is mauve.

Aileen La Tourette

Born US 1946. Holds world record in Catholic education (16 years). Has been most things, in one form or another (except Pope). Is still a mother, a writer, a firmly uncloseted dyke after several false starts. *Weddings and Funerals* book of short stories co-authored with Sara Maitland (Brilliance Books 1984); first novel, *Nuns and Mothers* (Virago 1984); second novel *Cry Wolf* (Virago 1986). Working on third novel and a collection of poems with photos by Phil Nice, *Grit for Icy Roads* and a collection of short stories *Ghosts In Aspic* which is still slightly spectral.

Suniti Namjoshi

was born in Bombay, India in 1941. Her books include *The Jackass and the Lady*; *Feminist Fables*; *The Authentic Lie*; *From The Bedside Book of Nightmares*; *The Conversations of Cow*; *Aditi and the One-Eyed Monkey*; and *Flesh and Paper* (with Gillian Hanscombe). She teaches at Scarborough College, University of Toronto.

Jan Parker

was born in London in 1957 and was sparked into political activity by the student Left in 1976. She is an independent socialist, a feminist and (need it be said in this context?) a lesbian – not necessarily in that order. She was a member of NUS Women's Committee 1977-79 and then office worker for the Campaign Against the Corrie Bill and the National Abortion Campaign. A former member of the Spare Rib collective, she stills writes and harbours a fantasy about being a singer. She worked until 1986 in the GLC Women's Committee Support Unit. Destination unknown: no doubt la lotta continua.

Alan Wakeman

Published work ranges from an English language course that sold all over the world, through photographic essays of London, to short stories, plays and children's books. His play *Ships* was in the season that launched Gay Sweatshop in 1975. When it was suggested that the group should have a display in the foyer, he painted his thoughts on heterosexuality directly onto the wall of the theatre virtually word for word as they are reproduced here. His most recent work, *The Vegan Cookbook* (with Gordon Baskerville), was published by Faber in 1986.

Jon Ward

was born in 1950 and lives in London. His published work includes the short story 'Dear Mrs Ashe' in *Cracks in the Image* (GMP 1981); a text-book, *Write Better English* (Cambridge University Press); and a book for young children, *Big Baby* illustrated by Claudio Muñoz (Walker Books). He is currently completing for GMP a book-length essay, *Unspeakable Desire*.

Books by and for women from GMP:

Brigid Brophy
The Finishing Touch

Comedy ensues when a disaster hits an exclusive girls' finishing school on the French Riviera. A classic novel from 'a brilliant stylist' – *Evening Standard*.

Kay Dick
The Shelf

A lesbian mystery set in the 1960s. 'Theme, manner and writing evoke Colette' – *The Times*.

Michael Baker
Our Three Selves

The acclaimed biography of lesbian novelist Radclyffe Hall.

Susanne Bösche
Jenny Lives With Eric and Martin

The controversial story in pictures of a 6-year-old girl who lives with her daddy and his lover.

Kate Charlesworth
Exotic Species

Razor-sharp ornithological cartoons of lesbian and gay types.

in Heretic Books

Pat Arrowsmith
Jericho

A novel of the peace camps, set in the 1950s.

Kath Clements
Why Vegan

Examines the moral, political and economic reasons for ending exploitation of animals.

Kit Mouat
Fighting For Our Lives

A book on the pioneering work of Cancer Contact, the mutual aid network.